Geospatial Law, Policy and Ethics

This comprehensive textbook identifies the emerging legal, policy, and ethical considerations associated with the collection, analysis, storage, and distribution of data that can be tied to location on Earth – otherwise known as "geospatial information."

Drawing on the author's extensive professional, legal, and scholarly experience in the geospatial community, the book explains how these issues cut across both legal and technology domains and how they impact geospatial information management across the globe. While focused on the USA, the framework and analysis can be applied to other nations and legal systems. Key topics covered include intellectual property, privacy, data protection, data quality and liability, security, ethical issues, licensing, and the impact of existing and emerging technologies, such as artificial intelligence, satellites, drones, software, machine learning, small satellites, and 5G. The book includes helpful features, such as a glossary of key legal terms and further reading, and is accompanied by digital supplements in the form of PowerPoint slides for each chapter.

Geospatial Law, Policy and Ethics is the ideal companion for advanced undergraduate and graduate-level students of Geographic Information System (GIS), remote sensing geospatial intelligence, geospatial studies, and spatial data science courses. It will also be of interest to geospatial professionals employed in industry, government, or research.

Kevin D. Pomfret is Partner at Williams Mullen law firm, Founder of the Centre for Spatial Law and Policy, and Professor of Geospatial Law.

Geospatial Law, Policy and Ethics

Where Geospatial Technology Is Taking the Law

Kevin D. Pomfret

Routledge
Taylor & Francis Group
LONDON AND NEW YORK

Designed cover image: Chor muang/Getty Images ®

First published 2025
by Routledge
4 Park Square, Milton Park, Abingdon, Oxon OX14 4RN

and by Routledge
605 Third Avenue, New York, NY 10158

Routledge is an imprint of the Taylor & Francis Group, an informa business

British Library Cataloguing-in-Publication Data
A catalogue record for this book is available from the British Library

ISBN: 978-1-032-36031-7 (hbk)
ISBN: 978-1-032-36028-7 (pbk)
ISBN: 978-1-003-32996-1 (ebk)

DOI: 10.4324/9781003329961

Typeset in Sabon
by Apex CoVantage, LLC

Access the Support Material: www.routledge.com/9781032360287

This book is dedicated to my beloved wife, Laura Delgado López, without whose unwavering support, encouragement, and love this book would not have been completed. To my children, Talene and KJ Pomfret, thank you for being on this journey with me since you were young.

Special thanks to Greg Scott, CheeHai Teo, and Yana Gevorgyan, as you supported my work on an international scale, expanding its reach beyond what I could have imagined. Posthumous thanks to Michael Jones, whose initial support and encouragement to explore the realms of geospatial law was invaluable.

Gratitude is also due to Scott Pace and Jack O'Connell, who encouraged my teaching in order to foster a deeper understanding and passion for geospatial policy and ethics in future generations of students.

This work builds upon the work of many others, including George Cho, Harlan Onsrud, and Bishop Dansby. Also, Rachael Scott, Catherine Ryan, and Bailey Cunningham provided critical research throughout the project.

I thank each of you for your pivotal role in the creation of this book. I could not have done it without you.

Contents

About the Author

Kevin D. Pomfret is a partner at the Williams Mullen law firm and the founder of the Centre for Spatial Law and Policy. He is recognized as the leading authority on the legal and policy issues that impact the collection, use, storage, and distribution of geospatial information, such as government and commercial contracts, privacy and data protection, data quality, and liability and regulatory matters.

Mr. Pomfret has testified at the U.S. Congressional hearings and presented at United Nations' committee meetings. He is a member of the U.S. Department of Commerce's Advisory Committee on Commercial Remote Sensing (ACCRES) and the UN-GGIM Working Group on Policy and Legal Frameworks for Geospatial Information Management. He is also an adjunct professor on geospatial law and ethics at Johns Hopkins University and regularly conducts training and workshops across the globe on legal and policy issues associated with geospatial information management.

Kevin has been recognized by Who's Who Legal as an outstanding lawyer in the transport – international space and satellites market, one of only a few attorneys in the U.S. selected for this honor and is regularly included in the list of *The Best Lawyers in America*©. Mr. Pomfret is a graduate of Washington and Lee School of Law and Bates College.

Mr. Pomfret began his career as a satellite imagery analyst with the National Photographic Interpretation Center. In that capacity he helped to develop imagery collection strategies and identify requirements for future collection systems.

Glossary of Key Legal Terms

Attribution: Crediting a piece of work (like a map or dataset) to the person or organization that created it.

Breach: Not following through on a promise in an agreement, especially in contracts.

Copyright: Legal protection for creators of original works, giving them exclusive rights to use and distribute their work for a certain period.

Data Sovereignty: The concept that digital data is subject to the laws of the country in which it is located. Geospatial information collected in one country may be governed by that country's laws, affecting its storage, transmission, and use.

Derivative Work: A new work created from one or more existing works, protected by copyright.

End-User License Agreement (EULA): A legal contract between the developer or publisher and the user, outlining the terms of use and distribution.

Fair Use: A legal doctrine that permits limited use of copyrighted material without requiring permission from the rights holders, under certain conditions.

FOIA (Freedom of Information Act): A law that gives you the right to access information from the federal government.

Force Majeure: Unforeseeable events outside human control, like natural disasters, preventing a party from fulfilling a contract.

Indemnification: A promise to cover the costs of damage or loss another party might suffer.

Intellectual Property (IP): A category of property that includes intangible creations of the human intellect, such as inventions; literary and artistic works; designs; and symbols, names, and images used in commerce.

Liability: Legal responsibility for something, arising from harm or damage.

License (Data Sharing) Agreement: Agreement that specifies how geospatial information can be used by others.

Licensee: The person or organization that receives a license.

Licensor: The person or organization that grants a license.

Patent: A form of intellectual property that gives its owner the legal right to exclude others from making, using, or selling an invention for a limited period of years in exchange for publishing an enabling public disclosure of the invention.

Product Liability: Legal responsibility for selling a defective product.

Public Domain: Works not protected by copyright and available for public use.

Publish: To make a work available to the public.

Representation: A factual statement made to persuade someone to enter a contract.

Trade Secret: Confidential business information that provides a competitive edge.

Trademark: A symbol, word, or words legally registered or established by use as representing a company or product.

Utility Patent: Patents that are granted for the invention or discovery of new and useful processes, machines, or compositions of matter, or any new and useful improvements thereof.

Warranty: A guarantee that a product or service will meet certain standards.

Work: Creative pieces like maps, datasets, or software.

1 What Is Geospatial Law?

Introduction

The purpose of this textbook is to guide the reader through the complex legal, policy, and ethical issues that impact geospatial information management. Geospatial information management is the collection, acquisition, use, analysis, visualization, storage, and distribution of the many different types of geospatial information – essentially data that can be associated with a location on Earth.[1] Geospatial law is an increasingly critical area of law due to the vast amounts of geospatial information that is being created or collected, and the role this information plays in a growing number of applications vital to government, industry, and society. In order for geospatial technology and the associated information to reach its vast potential, it is essential for geospatial professionals, whether in industry, government, or academia, to have an understanding of how these legal, policy, and ethical issues impact geospatial information so they can enhance the value of their geospatial assets, mitigate risk to themselves and their organizations, as well as to participate in the ongoing discussions on how to address the challenges posed by digital technologies more broadly.

This textbook is intended for current or aspiring geospatial professionals who are interested in the legal, policy, and ethical issues associated with the work they do. An understanding of the law is not required. The reader will see how, as in many other technology fields, geospatial information management is undergoing tremendous change. Perhaps the most significant change is the increase in technological advancements that have resulted in smaller sensors being placed more cheaply on a variety of platforms (i.e., satellites, smartphones, drones, Internet of Things (IoT) devices, and autonomous vehicles.) These sensors are collecting a wide range of geospatial information types that until recently were primarily limited to the defense and intelligence agencies of the most advanced countries. These include very high-resolution

1 See e.g., International Standards Organization TC 211. (n.d.). *Strategic plan*. Retrieved December 30, 2023, from www.isotc211.org/strategic-policy/.

DOI: 10.4324/9781003329961-1

electro-optical imagery, radar, infrared, LiDAR, and radio frequency data from satellites and drones, precise geolocation data from mobile devices and in situ data. Improvements in communications technology, adoption of standards for interoperability, and broad use of application program interfaces (APIs) now allows for the transfer of geospatial information almost seamlessly across the globe. Organizations of all types – government, industry, nongovernmental organizations (NGOs), research institutes, as well as criminal groups and terrorist cells – can then use advancements in computers, machine learning, and cloud architecture to process, analyze, and store this information quickly, easily, and at minimum cost. This information can then be aggregated with many other types of data, such as social media and government and business records, and analyzed by humans, but also increasingly through artificial intelligence. The results are then visualized on traditional maps, "Digital Twins" or in augmented or virtual reality (i.e., the "metaverse").

This book contains general, condensed summaries of actual legal matters, statutes, and opinions that are provided information purposes. It is not meant to be and should not be construed as legal advice.

Role of Geospatial Information

Geospatial information is now being used in every aspect of society. For example, government agencies around the world are repositories of vast quantities of geospatial information. Much of this information can be tied to a location (e.g., public transportation tables, road repairs and closings, tax and parcel records, neighborhood crime reports, street-cleaning schedules). Effective geospatial information management requires that this information be shared among government agencies to make "place-based" policy decisions. For example, deploying resources in those communities that have the most need and then being able to measure success. Accurate and timely geospatial information also can make citizens safer and improve services, thereby improving the quality of life in a community. For example, first responders can use geospatial information to notify citizens in real time of evacuation routes during emergencies, such as forest fires or flash foods. Similarly, law enforcement can use geospatial information to quickly identify and track criminal activity. Providing government services more quickly and efficiently can also reduce costs, which is an important consideration in times of budget constraints.

Businesses already aggregate geospatial information with other data types for a variety of commercial purposes. For example, the insurance industry uses geospatial information to both better assess risk and to pay out claims quicker. The retail industry has improved awareness of their customers by using geospatial information collected from mobile apps or the internet. Geospatial information is critical in both tracking business assets and for home delivery of groceries and food. Some farmers use this information to protect and more efficiently harvest crops, and the mining industry uses geospatial technology to identify natural resources. In fact, there is potential for many more applications, given the new data types that will be collected from space, air, and in situ.

Individuals now use applications that integrate geospatial information in a variety of ways, including navigation, social media, and protecting loved ones. Young people enjoy gaming platforms that use geospatial information for more realistic and interactive mobile and 3D experiences. Citizens can check the real-time status of public transportation from home before heading out to the bus or train station. They also can update and verify government information pertaining to them, their neighborhoods, streets, schools, etc., in real time.

Geospatial technology also allows citizens to become active participants in how their communities operate. They can notify government agencies of the location of crimes, public nuisances, accidents, or damage to public infrastructure with the simple click of a button on their mobile device. Government agencies can then process and respond to these notices, and citizens can then verify that appropriate action was taken.

As the previous discussion highlights, one of the unique aspects of geospatial information is that it is used by government agencies (civil and defense/intelligence), industry, and citizens alike. This versatility is one of the reasons this sector is so valuable. From an economic standpoint, the benefits range from commuting/fuel efficiency and safer travel for consumers to new products and services and increased productivity for businesses. For example, in a 2022 report, Geospatial World estimated that the size of the global geospatial market in 2030 will be $1.4 trillion.[2]

This textbook will explain how this versatility of geospatial information comes at a price, as it raises a number of complex legal, policy, and ethical challenges. In fact, this versatility is arguably holding back greater use of geospatial information across the geospatial ecosystem. For example, national security concerns restrict the collection of certain types of geospatial information and limit the export of sensitive geospatial technology, products, and services. Similarly, the impact of intellectual property rights, liability concerns, and increasingly laws that are intended to protect consumer privacy can limit the collection, use, and sharing of geospatial information.

The COVID-19 pandemic highlighted that the challenges facing humankind are not contained within a nation's borders. Issues such as (i) climate change, (ii) containing the spread of infectious diseases, (iii) managing the oceans' resources, and (iv) combating terrorism and piracy all require governments from across the globe to work together and share timely and

2 Geospatial World. (n.d.). *Advancing & augmenting USD 1.4 trillion geospatial market by 2030*. Retrieved December 30, 2023, from www.geospatialworld.net/latest/advancing-augmenting-usd-1-4-trillion-geospatial-market-by-2030/.

accurate geospatial information. Many countries wish to become leaders in geospatial information management to address critical issues, such as achieving the United Nations' Sustainable Development Goals (SDGs). However, while it is now possible from a technical standpoint to transfer geospatial information seamlessly from one country to another, non-technical hurdles exist as the legal frameworks in each country are very different. Differences in intellectual property rights, procurement, national security laws, privacy regulations, and governance can make it difficult to develop detailed, real-time models of the entire globe to address these issues.

Achieving many of these applications and the associated benefits will require organizations being able to safely and securely collect accurate, precise, and often sensitive information and aggregate it with other information from a variety of other sources. While the geospatial community is actively working to address the complex technical and operational challenges, it often minimizes the impact of legal and policy issues. The purpose of this book is to raise awareness of these challenges so they can be adequately addressed.

Unique Aspects of Geospatial Information From a Legal Standpoint

Some of the legal and ethical issues discussed in this book naturally arise with all new technologies or applications, as the legal and policy communities generally are reactive rather than proactive. The geospatial ecosystem (i.e., government, industry, academia, NGOs, private citizens) will also be subject to the larger legal and policy issues that are being raised by the increase in "Big Data." While the geospatial community has been "Big Data" before Big Data was cool, little attention was paid to the legal and policy issues. This will need to change, as lawmakers and regulators are increasingly focused on issues such as privacy, liability, and the national security implications of technologies that are deemed "dual use" (i.e., can be used for civil/commercial as well as military/intelligence applications), as is the case with many geospatial technologies. This book will explain the impact these new laws and policies will have on the geospatial ecosystem.

The geospatial community often asks whether "spatial is special." The purpose of this textbook is to show how, at least from a legal and policy standpoint, the answer is clearly "yes." There are several unique aspects of geospatial information that must be considered. These include the following:

- The Geospatial Community Is an Ecosystem – As stated previously, the geospatial community is an ecosystem consisting of a variety of stakeholders. These stakeholders include the following:

  Government Agencies – Government agencies at all levels (national, regional, and local) are significant stakeholders in geospatial information management. Some of these, such as agencies responsible for land registry/cadastral, land planning, national mapping, and spatial data infrastructures (SDIs) are traditionally associated with geospatial information management. Solving most government problems requires aggregating different datasets from a variety of government agencies. However, as this textbook will explain, even sharing geospatial information between agencies within the same country is challenging, often due to the legal and policy issues associated with geospatial information. In fact, one government agency may use the legal and policy uncertainty to justify not sharing with another agency, even if the real reason is to maintain control, or to not incur the additional expense. These issues become even more complex as now most government agencies collect or use some type of geospatial information, often without recognizing the importance of such geospatial information in their decision-making or the services that they provide. Therefore, they do not always appreciate the need for data sharing.

Industry – Businesses of all types have regularly collected and used geospatial information in their operations. This includes information regarding the physical world, their customers, and employees as well their business assets, etc., as part of their day-to-day operations. This trend has increased as it has become easier, and cheaper, to collect and analyze geospatial information. However, recently the private sector has begun playing a larger role in collecting geospatial information to sell to governments, other businesses, and consumers. These range from satellite companies collecting Earth observation data, to companies aggregating and analyzing precise geolocation data collected from mobile devices. Analytics companies take this information and run it through software to visualize the results, identify patterns or unique insights or as a tip-off to collect new data. Many of these businesses have raised a great deal of money from outside investors, such as venture capital funds. These inventors expect a return on their investment (ROI). As industry continues to collect, create, and ingest growing amounts of geospatial information, the legal and ethical issues become more complicated and more important. For example, Chapter 2 will explain how businesses are concerned about protecting their intellectual property rights to increase their ROI. Chapter 9 will explain how procurement rules and government regulations make it challenging for many government agencies to procure geospatial products and services from the private sector.

Citizens – In the past, a citizen's primary role with respect to geospatial information was as a recipient. For example, a citizen might have benefited from geospatial-enabled services that a government agency provided, such as transportation services or land information or records. However, technology has now made it possible for citizens also to become collectors of geospatial information. They are both using this information in their daily lives as well as sharing it with other stakeholders in the ecosystem. (i.e., government agencies, the private sector,

NGOs, and other citizens). As will be discussed, the U.S. legal system has specific laws that protect individuals to a greater extent than businesses. For example, laws that protect privacy are becoming more common as geospatial technology becomes more ubiquitous. In addition, this book will explain how the increased role of citizens in geospatial information management raises complex ethical issues.

Universities/Nongovernmental Organizations (NGOs) – Universities, NGOs, and research organizations are significant consumers of geospatial information, particularly in addressing transnational issues such as climate change, conservation, and the SDGs. Much of the geospatial information necessary for this work is provided by government agencies at no or little cost. However, the growing role of the private sector in areas traditionally served by government is adding to the complexity of these relationships as companies wish to charge for these products and services. This sector of the ecosystem also is directly collecting more geospatial information from citizens through such means as "crowdsourcing" or using small satellites and drones. In some instances, these organizations are even competing with the private sector.

As noted previously, each stakeholder in the ecosystem can play the role of a data collector and data user: sometimes at the same time. This book will explain how laws and policies that are designed to regulate the collection or use of geospatial information by one sector of the ecosystem will often have an impact on the other sectors. For example, in some cases government agencies are now directed by law to use the private sector to the greatest extent possible when considering acquiring geospatial information. Laws that limit the private sector's ability to collect geospatial information may result in less information being available for government use. Similarly, limiting the ability of government to collect or share certain types of geospatial information due to privacy concerns likely will result in agencies not being able to provide services that could be used to improve citizens' lives or other societal benefits, such as monitoring the impact of climate change.

- Geospatial Information Is Diverse – The term geospatial information can be used to define a wide range of data types, such as addresses, surveys, electro-optical satellite imagery, LIDAR from autonomous platforms, precise geolocation information from mobile devices, and geo-tagged photos or posts from a social media application. By way of example, there are 18 data themes and 173 different datasets that comprise the National Geospatial Data Asset Portfolio in the U.S.[3] In addition, geospatial information is

3 Federal Geographic Data Committee. (n.d.). *A-16 NGDA portfolio management.* Retrieved December 30, 2023, from www.fgdc.gov/what-we-do/manage-federal-geospatial-resources/a-16-portfolio-management/ngda-themes-and-datasets.

collected from a variety of sensors, mounted on many different platforms, including drones flown by a commercial enterprise, citizens using GPS-enabled mobile devices in their spare time and government surveyors mapping a forest.

This book will explain how the legal and ethical issues can vary greatly between these datasets. In addition, definitions are very important in any legal context, whether it be a law, a contract, or a court case. This book will explain why it will be critical in legal settings to carefully define different types of geospatial technologies and information. For example, defining what types of geospatial information are subject to export restrictions due to national security concerns, without being overly broad so as to inadvertently restrict the exchange of geospatial information needed to address critical transnational issues. Perhaps even more importantly will be having a legal and policy framework in place that makes it clear which agency is responsible for making that decision within the U.S. government for which types of geospatial technology or information.

- Geospatial Information Is Versatile – Geospatial information is used for many different applications. For example, geospatial information is critical in (i) providing turn-by-turn navigation, (ii) understanding the impact of CO^2 emissions around the globe, (iii) assessing and managing risks, such as water scarcity or deforestation, and (iv) planning national infrastructure projects. Moreover, a single geospatial information dataset can be used by several different actors for a variety of different purposes. For example, a school's location can be used by a state's Department of Education for planning bus routes, as well as by first responders for evacuation planning during an emergency. However, the same information can also be used by those wishing to harm children. Any legal or regulatory effort that attempts to limit the availability of geospatial information (e.g., the school's location or its entry/exit points) to protect against improper activities could reduce the availability or use of the same information for a proper purpose (e.g., by a first responder).

In addition, even if geospatial information can be used for one application, it may not be suited for that application. For example, a dataset of geospatial information may be suitable for mapping but not have the accuracy, the timeliness, or the completeness for real-time decision-making. Someone who does not have a background in data science or who does not fully understand geospatial information may not be aware of these limitations. This risk of misuse – and the associated liability issues – increases as geospatial information management is pushed deeper into organizations.

- Geospatial-related Issues Cut Across a Variety of Technology Platforms – Geospatial information is generated from a variety of technologies, including mapping and surveying tools, global navigation satellite systems (GNSS), remote sensing (both aerial and satellite), smartphones, and radio frequency identification (RFID). The geospatial information that is collected with these technologies is used in diverse industries, each with their own business models, objectives, risks, and even vernacular. Currently, different federal agencies regulate distinct technologies or platforms associated with the collection or use of geospatial information. Each agency has been given this regulatory authority under different legislation and often has different perspectives on the benefits and/or risks of geospatial information. For example, the Federal Aviation Administration (FAA), the primary regulator for drones, has different roles and responsibilities from the National Oceanic and Atmospheric Administration (NOAA), which is responsible for licensing commercial imaging satellites, or the Federal Trade Commission (FTC), which is responsible for protecting consumers from the privacy risks associated with the collection of location information. Each of these agencies can have an impact on the use of geospatial information, and an organization that wishes to aggregate data across platforms must at least consider the applicability of regulations and policies of all three (and many others). In addition, which will be discussed in more detail, state agencies also play an important role in some geospatial sectors.

- Different Laws and Regulations Impact the Geospatial Sector – There are numerous laws and policies that can impact geospatial information management. Some of these apply to specific aspects of the process. For example, surveying in the United States is generally regulated by state authorities, while the Federal Geospatial Data Act of 2018 pertains to the development of the U.S. national spatial data infrastructure. In addition, there are several legal domains, including laws pertaining to contracts (government and commercial), intellectual property rights, government procurement, exports, liability, and privacy laws that while not unique to the collection and use of geospatial information, nonetheless have a significant impact and must be considered.
- Geospatial Technology Is Rapidly Changing – The technology for the collection, use, storage, and distribution of geospatial information is rapidly changing. The legal community is not suited to keep up with this pace of change as law is by nature, if not intent, meant to be reactive, not proactive. As a result, there often are gaps as to how a law applies to a particular technology, application, or data type. As lawmakers and regulators in the U.S. begin to address the complex legal issues associated with geospatial technology, laws, policies, and regulations related to geospatial information likely will undergo significant change. In the meantime, lawyers and their clients will struggle with what is permitted under law and the associated risks of failing to comply.
- The Government Plays Multiple Roles in the Geospatial Ecosystem – Although the geospatial ecosystem is diverse, the U.S. government plays

an outsized role. Therefore, it is important to understand the various capacities played by the U.S. government as well as the myriad of associated legal and policy issues.

Government as a data collector – Federal, state, and local government agencies collect a vast amount of geospatial information for civil, defense, and intelligence purposes and for scientific use. In addition, the National Reconnaissance Office (NRO), NOAA, and the National Aeronautics and Space Administration (NASA) each operate satellites that collect Earth observation data. While much of the information collected by civil agencies (i.e., NASA and NOAA) is used to meet specific agency missions, because geospatial information is so versatile it can also be used by other stakeholders, including scientists and industry. As a result, there are requirements for government agencies to make this information available to other agencies, the private sector, research institutions, and even internationally at no cost. However, making this data freely and openly available can be challenging from a legal standpoint. For example, in some instances by providing this information, government agencies are competing with the private sector. In addition, as will be discussed later, "open data" policies are often interpreted to apply to geospatial information procured by governmental agencies from the private sector. Making this information broadly available for free limits the ability for the commercial sector to sell to the other customers in the geospatial market.

Government as a customer – Federal, state, and local agencies are also significant purchasers of all types of geospatial products and services. The U.S. Department of Defense and the U.S. Intelligence Community are likely the largest customer of geospatial products and services in the world, through purchases of hardware (e.g., satellites, sensors, and drones), data (e.g., satellite remote sensing and aerial data) and software, and associated services and solutions. NOAA, and the Departments of Transportation, Agriculture, and Interior are also significant customers, as is the Census Bureau in the Department of Commerce. At the state and local levels, government agencies use geospatial products and services for urban planning, transportation, and law enforcement. As will be discussed in Chapter 9, many segments of the geospatial ecosystem are therefore reliant upon the government market and thus subject to its complex procurement laws and policies.

Government as a regulator – As will be discussed in Chapter 8, the government also serves the role of a regulator in geospatial information management. For example, the launch and operation of commercial remote sensing satellites are regulated by NOAA, the Federal Aviation Administration (FAA), and the Federal Communications Commission (FCC). Human-operated aircraft and drones are regulated by the FAA, while the privacy concerns associated with drones are regulated by the FTC.

> Collection and use of geospatial information by the federal government is covered by numerous laws and policies, such as the Geospatial Data Act of 2018. States regulate the activities of surveyors. In addition, numerous states have restrictions on data collection by drones.

This book will explain how these myriads of laws, regulations, and policies impact geospatial information management with the U.S. It includes chapters on the legal framework with respect to the government's use of geospatial information for defense and intelligence purposes (GEOINT), and by federal, state, and local government agencies for civil purposes. It will also include a chapter on selling geospatial products and services to the U.S. government.

Legal Considerations

This book will explain how there are many legal issues that impact geospatial information management within the U.S. Some are more traditional legal issues that must be considered regarding any technology. These include the following:

- Intellectual Property Rights. Geospatial products and services are increasingly created by combining geospatial information from a variety of sources. However, Chapter 2 will discuss how the intellectual property rights in geospatial information are often different than in other non-tangible assets, such as software. For example, in the U.S. copyright law generally protects maps and images, however it does not apply to facts or "information," unless the data is creatively organized. Consequently, there is some uncertainty with how to apply such rights to geospatial information that is posted on the internet, or generated automatically, such as through the IoT. It is also unclear what level of protection courts will grant owners of geospatial information collected from the numerous types of sensors that are becoming more commercially viable. In addition, federal government agencies cannot claim copyright in information and products they create. However, some states do allow their agencies to claim copyright, which must be taken into consideration for example when developing a map of the U.S. by combining federal and state data.
- Privacy/Data Protection. Chapter 3 will highlight the growing trend across the U.S. to regulate the collection and use of personal information that could be used to harm an individual or infringe upon his or her privacy. Historically, most geospatial information has not been considered personal information. However, lawmakers and regulators are recognizing that many types of geospatial information are a powerful tool to identify an individual, either directly or indirectly through, for example, a mobile device. Such concerns become even greater when datasets of otherwise non-personal geospatial information are aggregated due to concerns that

such aggregation can identify an individual. As a result, the federal government is taking steps to protect this information. In the meantime, laws are being passed at the state level to regulate the collection and use of certain types of geospatial information.

- Data Quality/Liability. As described previously, geospatial information is very versatile. A single dataset can be used in a variety of applications. However, although a dataset is capable of being used in an application, it may not be suitable for such use. For example, the dataset may not be accurate or precise enough, or it may be incomplete or outdated for a particular application. Moreover, as decision-making around data use is distributed across organizations, the people making the decisions may not have sufficient understanding of data science, or the various components of data quality, to make informed decisions. The challenge becomes even more complex as decisions are being made based upon data that is received, processed, and used in near real-time. Chapter 4 will explain how under U.S. law, the legal requirements for a data provider from a liability standpoint can vary depending upon whether the data is considered a product or a service. While organizations can mitigate some of these risks through disclaimers in contracts, as will be discussed, in some instances the law will provide that such disclaimers do not apply.
- National Security. In the U.S., as in many parts of the world, geospatial technology was initially developed and used for defense and national security purposes. As a result, agencies within those sectors of the U.S. government approach geospatial information with a great deal of ambivalence. On the one hand, parts of these agencies see tremendous value in acquiring as much geospatial information as possible. Other parts of the same agency, however, will be concerned about the data ending up in the hands of adversaries.

As a result, there are ongoing efforts to prohibit or restrict the collection and/or distribution of geospatial information for national security purposes. In some instances, such as the licensing requirements for commercial remote sensing or export control restrictions – these have been placed into law. However, these restrictions can also take the form of policies, both formal and informal. Adding to the complexity is the ever-changing geopolitical environment, in which geospatial information is both a tool and a weapon. In the U.S. this has created an increasingly complex legal regime for dealing with the U.S. government. While the U.S. government defense and intelligence communities are a compelling market for geospatial products and services, this book will show some of the challenges faced, particularly by smaller companies, in navigating the complex security obligations.

- Cybersecurity. Cybersecurity is an evolving area of law that will increasingly have an impact on geospatial information management. As geospatial information becomes more valuable, the need to protect it grows.

> Geospatial organizations increasingly will be required to comply with security measures imposed by laws and regulations that are intended to protect sensitive information – even if the information is not considered classified. Similarly, many states have laws that require organizations to notify government agencies and/or individuals if personal information has been lost or stolen, such as through a data breach, or otherwise improperly accessed. Many of these are also imposing their own cybersecurity requirements, particularly in the finance and health sectors.

Many of the most powerful applications using geospatial information require aggregating different types of geospatial information collected from a variety of sensors and platforms from across the geospatial ecosystem. This will require one party agreeing to share (or license) geospatial information with another party, typically accomplished through a license or data sharing agreement, which can take many forms. As will be discussed in Chapter 7, a data sharing/license agreement serves several important purposes. One purpose is to transfer the rights to use geospatial information. However, these agreements also play an important role in allocating risks between the parties associated with the legal issues discussed in this book. For example, a well-crafted agreement will address which party is responsible if a third party is injured from a product or service using the licensed geospatial information, or what are the respective party's obligations to comply with applicable privacy laws. These are important considerations because if the parties decide not to address them in an agreement, they are leaving it up to a third party – that is, jury, judge, regulator – to decide in the event of a dispute.

Ethical Considerations

Broader adoption of geospatial technology also raises ethical issues. One common issue is geospatial information may be collected for use for one purpose, but easily repurposed either alone or with other data, in a way that many people would consider sensitive or embarrassing. For example, an NGO may collect geospatial information to assist local communities in building medical facilities, but a government agency may use the same information to monitor the activities of certain individuals in that community. Also, there are ethical issues around the accuracy and completeness of the data. For example, if a dataset to be used to train an algorithm is not representative of an entire community, the results may be skewed. This can result in poor policy decisions, or even discrimination. For the reasons set forth previously, information security can also be an ethical issue. It is important to make sure that sensitive data is protected when transmitted and stored, even if not required under law. This includes having policies in place to retain data only as long as is necessary and to properly delete the information when the purpose for which it was originally collected or acquired had ended.

As discussed in Chapter 8, several challenges exist when it comes to applying ethics to the geospatial ecosystem. These include the following:

- *Expansive geospatial ecosystem* – A broad geospatial ecosystem makes it difficult to develop a code of ethics that can be universally applied. The ethical issues faced by a software engineer are very different than those faced by a drone operator, or a surveyor. Similarly, government employees have different ethical obligations than those in the private industry.
- *Numerous other stakeholders* – There are many stakeholders that are collecting or using geospatial information who do not consider themselves part of the geospatial community; for example, organizations and individuals who work in the autonomous vehicle industry. They are not likely to even consider that a geospatial code of ethics should apply to them. In fact, some may be subject to other distinct codes of ethics.
- *Ethics vs law* – It is important to make a proper distinction between law and ethics. For example, it would be a mistake to focus solely on the ethical considerations associated with location privacy without understanding the legal obligations associated with data protection/privacy. In general ethics should be obligations that an organization should take in addition to its legal requirements, not replace them.

Conclusion and How to Use This Book

Users of this book should come away with the understanding the impact that geospatial technology and applications using geospatial information are having from a legal standpoint in addition to the economic and societal impacts. The book begins with a discussion of key areas of law and how these apply to geospatial information management. Key issues discussed include intellectual property rights, privacy, liability, national security, as well as regulatory matters. These chapters will include reference to U.S. laws and regulations as well as relevant court cases in which these issues have been raised.

It then discusses how these issues impact the licensing of geospatial information as well as the ethical issues that arise. The reader will better understand the roles of licenses and ethics and the close relationship between each and the legal issues addressed in the early chapters.

The remainder of the book discusses the U.S. government's role in geospatial information management. This includes the complexities involved in the federal government's procurement of geospatial products and services from the private sector. Also discussed are some of the key laws and policies that impact geospatial information management by both civil agencies as well as the defense/intelligence sector of the U.S. government.

The book is structured to be used as a textbook; however it can also be used by geospatial professionals interested in having a better understanding of the key legal issues that impact their work. Of note to both students and professionals, there is a growing gap between the value of the geospatial sector and the legal framework as technology is evolving more quickly than the law can keep up. For example, developments in artificial intelligence and digital twins will certainly have legal and ethical implications. Many of the issues will not be unique to geospatial, but the legal solutions to address them almost certainly will impact the geospatial community, likely in some ways that are not intended. The intent of this book is to provide a baseline and structure to understand the impact these developments likely will have on the geospatial community.

Also of note is that the geospatial community is inherently international. This book focuses on U.S. law, but geospatial information is often collected in one part of the world, transferred in real-time to another country where it is processed and used to create products and services that are then used in another country. The legal and policy frameworks in each of these countries will differ, sometimes in significant ways. However, as most of the legal and ethical issues raised in in these chapters will apply in other countries, this book can provide a systematic approach to understand the impact those laws and policies have on geospatial information management.

2 Intellectual Property Rights in Geospatial

Introduction

As the value of the geospatial sector has increased, organizations have become more aware of the intellectual property rights associated with both geospatial technology and geospatial information. This chapter will discuss how in many instances intellectual property rights in the geospatial sector are very similar to those in other technology sectors. This is particularly true with respect to hardware and software. However, in other aspects, the geospatial sector is on the cutting edge of intellectual property law, particularly regarding data rights. This can result in uncertainty, which can make sharing of geospatial information more challenging than many expect when developing geospatial information products and services. As a result, it has become increasingly important for geospatial professionals to understand intellectual property law in general and the unique intellectual property issues associated with geospatial information.

What Are Intellectual Property Rights?

Intellectual property rights are legal rights, granted by a government, to protect creations (or works) of the human mind.[1] These include inventions, literary and artistic works, symbols, names, images, and designs. These rights are intended to provide the creators (or those to whom they have assigned their intellectual property rights) with exclusive rights to benefit from the works. Examples include the right to prevent others from using or exploiting the work without their permission.

Intellectual property rights are considered an important tool for incentivizing innovation, creativity, and investment. However, as will be described in further detail later, there is a tension inherent in intellectual property law between allowing creators to benefit from their creations and allowing the

1 See e.g., World Trade Organization. (n.d.). *What are intellectual property rights?* Retrieved December 30, 2023, from www.wto.org/english/tratop_e/trips_e/intel1_e.htm.

DOI: 10.4324/9781003329961-2

public to build upon this creativity, so as to fuel both technological innovation and scientific progress. Consequently, intellectual property rights often are limited to a defined period of time. Thereafter, others are free to create new technology, products, or services based upon the original work.

Intellectual property rights play a crucial role in geospatial information management. Geospatial information is often created through significant investments in technology and people and therefore represents a key asset for many organizations. Intellectual property rights help to protect these investments so that organizations can realize a return on investment and by implication, continue to invest in the development of new geospatial technology or geospatial information. As this chapter will explain though, this tension between protecting the rights of a creator versus the public good is particularly strong with respect to geospatial information.

There are two primary reasons why understanding intellectual property rights should be important to all geospatial professionals. First, since many geospatial products and services are protected by intellectual property rights, geospatial professionals need to be aware of these legal protections to prevent unintentional infringement on the rights of others and avoiding legal conflicts (i.e., litigation). Second, geospatial professionals are often involved in the creation, development, and distribution of geospatial information and software, which may be subject to intellectual property protections. An understanding of the types of, and requirements for, intellectual property rights can help professionals protect the value of the products and services they have created.

Types of Intellectual Property

This chapter will discuss several major types of intellectual property rights: patents, copyright, trade secrets, and trade/service marks. Each is important to geospatial organizations.

- *Patents.* The authority of the U.S. Patent and Trademark Office (USPTO) to grant patents is set forth in the United States Code.[2] There are two types of patents that are generally applicable to the geospatial community. These are utility patents and design patents.

  Utility patents. Utility patents are the most frequently issued type of patents. They are issued for new and useful innovations that include processes, machines, and novel improvements. For a geospatial organization, this might include specialized software programs, certain geospatial information analysis techniques, and novel surveying equipment. The lifespan of a utility patent typically is twenty (20) years. To qualify for a

2 Title 35, U.S. Code.

utility patent, the invention must meet several requirements, including being novel, non-obvious, and useful. Elements of usefulness include having a functional purpose that can be demonstrated and has some social benefit.

Design patents. Design patents are not as common as utility patents. They are issued in connection with new, original, and ornamental designs that are contained within or applied to something that is manufactured. They generally are considered easier and less expensive to obtain than a utility patent. However, they generally only last for fifteen (15) years.

- *Copyrights*. Copyright can protect literary, dramatic, musical, artistic, and other intellectual creations. Copyright grants the creator several exclusive rights, including the right to (i) reproduce the copyrighted work in copies; (ii) prepare derivative works based upon the copyrighted work; (iii) distribute copies of the copyrighted work to the public by sale or other transfer of ownership, or by rental, lease, or lending; (iv) perform the copyrighted work; and (v) display the copyrighted work publicly.[3]

Notably for the geospatial sector, copyright applies to software and many types of digital content. While patents must be formally registered in order to obtain protection under U.S. law, copyright protection is automatically granted upon creation of the work in a fixed, tangible form. However, registration with the U.S. Copyright Office provides several legal advantages, such as establishing a public record of the copyright claim. In addition, copyright registration is necessary to be eligible for statutory damages in infringement suits. The length of copyright protection varies, but for works created by an individual after January 1, 1978, copyright generally lasts for the life of the author plus seventy (70) years.

As will be discussed in further detail later, it is important for geospatial professionals to understand the concept of "fair use" under copyright law. Fair use permits limited use of copyrighted material without permission from the owner. These purposes include criticism, commentary, news reporting, teaching, scholarship, or research. Unfortunately, there are no specific rules regarding fair use. Factors in determining whether a use qualifies as fair use includes the purpose of the use, the nature of the copyrighted work, the amount used in relation to the work as a whole, and the impact on the market value of the work.[4]

Geospatial professionals must be cognizant of copyright law not only for works that they create but also when using third-party software (and in some instances, information). As will be discussed elsewhere in the book, this often requires complying with terms of an associated license or other agreement.

3 U.S. Copyright Act, codified at 17 U.S.C. §§ 101–810.
4 7 U.S. Code § 107.

Trade secrets. In the U.S., a company can protect proprietary information provided (i) the information has some economic benefit and (ii) the company has made a reasonable effort to maintain the secrecy of the information. As long as the secrecy is maintained and the information continues to generate economic value, a trade secret can potentially last indefinitely. The formula for Coke is often used as an example of a trade secret. For geospatial professionals, trade secrets could range from proprietary methods to unique business strategies.

Historically, trade secrets were protected at the state level. The Uniform Law Commission – an organization that aims to provide states with nonpartisan legislation on critical areas of law for clarity and stability – published the Uniform Trade Secrets Act (UTSA), a standardized legal framework for protecting trade secrets. The USTA includes remedies for misappropriation. It has almost been universally adopted by states. The Defend Trade Secrets Act (DTSA) became law in 2016 and provides statutory protection of trade secrets at the federal level.[5]

Protecting trade secrets is crucial for a geospatial organization as it helps to protect their proprietary data, technologies, and methodologies. It also helps remind employees to respect others' trade secrets, which reduces legal disputes.

- *Trademarks*. U.S. trademark law protects names, logos, slogans, and other marks that identify and distinguish a company's goods or services.[6] (If the identified offering is a service instead of a product, the mark is called a service mark). McDonald's Golden Arches is an example of a trademark. For geospatial professionals, a trademark could be the name of a geospatial software, a unique logo of a mapping company, or a distinct tagline associated with a company name.

Trademarks are secured simply by using them in the market. However, registering a trademark with the USPTO provides significant legal benefits. For example, registration helps to establish a public claim of ownership, making a claim of infringement easier. Unlike patents and copyrights, trademarks can be renewed indefinitely as long as they are being used and measures are taken to protect their distinctiveness. Such measures would include challenging any third-party's use of the trademark.

Legal Framework for Intellectual Property

As in many aspects of geospatial information management, the legal and policy framework for intellectual property rights has elements of international, national, and contract law.

5 18 U.S.C. § 1836, et seq.
6 Lanham Act codified at 15 U.S.C. §§ 1051 et seq.

International Law

As the geospatial ecosystem is international, it is important for many organizations to understand how intellectual property rights are protected in other countries. While as noted previously, intellectual property is protected at the national level, governments recognized that there was a need for coordination among nations. As a result, over the years there have been several treaties addressing intellectual property rights. The U.S. is a signatory to many of these treaties, including the following:

- The Berne Convention for the Protection of Literary and Artistic Works – The Berne Convention provides a framework for international cooperation and harmonization in copyright law.[7]
- The Paris Convention for the Protection of Industrial Property – The Paris Convention provides a framework for international cooperation in the protection of intellectual property rights, including rules for filing and granting of patents and trademarks, as well as provisions for enforcement and dispute resolution.[8]
- The Agreement on Trade-Related Aspects of Intellectual Property Rights – The TRIPS Agreement sets out minimum standards for intellectual property protection and enforcement for a wide range of intellectual property rights, including patents, trademarks, copyrights, and trade secrets.[9]
- The World Intellectual Property Organization Copyright Treaty – The WIPO Copyright Treaty extended the scope of the Berne Convention to include digital works and online distribution. It provides for protection of digital works such as software, music, and films, and requires countries to provide legal protection for technological measures used to protect these works.[10]

National Law

As noted previously, there are several federal laws that address intellectual property rights in the U.S. In addition to the laws listed previously, other

7 World Intellectual Property Organization. (n.d.). *Berne convention for the protection of literary and artistic works*. Retrieved December 30, 2024, from www.wipo.int/wipolex/en/treaties/textdetails/12214.

8 World Intellectual Property Organization. (n.d.). *Paris convention for the protection of industrial property*. Retrieved December 30, 2023, from www.wipo.int/treaties/en/ip/paris/.

9 World Trade Organization. (n.d.). *Agreement on trade-related aspects of intellectual property rights*. Retrieved December 30, 2023, from www.wto.org/english/docs_e/legal_e/27-trips_01_e.htm.

10 World Intellectual Property Organization. (n.d.). *WIPO Copyright Treaty (WCT)*. Retrieved December 30, 2023, from www.wipo.int/treaties/en/ip/wct/#:~:text=The%20WIPO%20Copyright%20Treaty%20%28WCT%29%20is%20a%20special,Berne%20Convention%2C%20they%20are%20granted%20certain%20economic%20rights.

important laws for geospatial professionals involving intellectual property rights include the following:

- *Digital Millennium Copyright Act* – The DMCA amended the Copyright Act to provide (i) legal remedies for copyright infringement on the internet and (ii) safe harbor protections for certain internet service providers and hosts.[11]
- *Computer Fraud and Abuse Act* – The CFAA prohibits unauthorized access to computers and networks, shielding sensitive information from cyber threats.[12]

Contract Law

Another legal method to protect intellectual property is through contracts. Geospatial organizations often need to share intellectual property with organizations. For example, businesses will share intellectual property rights in software when working with another business to develop an integrated software solution for a third party. Or a business may license geospatial information from another party to aggregate it with its own data to create a map to post on its website for customers.

Each of these relationships, and many others, requires an agreement between the parties that sets forth what intellectual property rights are being granted and the penalties for failing to comply with those rights. For example, if rights in a trade secret are being granted, the agreement should include a specific requirement that the party receiving the trade secret keep the information confidential. Otherwise the information may lose its status as a trade secret. Alternatively, there may be a requirement for a party receiving software that is subject to copyright to maintain all copyright markings.

If other technology sectors are an example, as the geospatial ecosystem grows, there is likely to be an increasing number of lawsuits to protect patents, copyright, and trade secrets. These lawsuits can be very expensive for both parties involved as they often take several years to be resolved, and the awarded damages can be large.

Unique Intellectual Property Issues in Geospatial Information Management

As noted previously, many of the issues associated with intellectual property rights are not unique to geospatial organizations. For example, technology companies of all types often consider whether to patent new hardware. However, there are several unique issues associated with geospatial information with regards to intellectual property.

11 Public Law 105–304–OCT. 28, 1998.
12 18 U.S. Code § 1030.

Limited Copyright Protection

One important consideration is that geospatial information receives much less copyright protection than geospatial software. The courts have found that there is no creativity involved in collecting or compiling facts, so copyright protection generally does not apply.

The seminal case on this issue was *Feist v. Rural Telephone Service*, a Supreme Court case from 1991.[13] In that case Feist had copied a telephone directory published by Rural Telephone Service containing the names and telephone numbers of residents in a community. Rural Telephone sued Feist, claiming it had violated Rural Telephone's copyright in its telephone directory. The Supreme Court held that the names and telephone numbers were facts, and because there was no creativity[14] or innovation involved in compiling the information, the information itself was not copyrightable. The Court also found that as the only logical way to organize a telephone directory was alphabetically, by name, there was no creativity in how the facts were organized and consequently no copyright protection applied in the compilation as a whole. Since the decision in *Feist*, at least a modicum of creativity is required in terms of how a database was created or the facts organized in order to receive copyright protection for a database.

Unfortunately, the requisite level of creativity for copyright in facts has not been clearly defined in case law. As a result, the court cases involving these issues are very fact specific. For example, in *Alexandria Drafting v. Amsterdam*, Alexandria Drafting claimed that Amsterdam (doing business as Franklin Maps) copied its map book in violation of the Copyright Act.[15] According to the facts set forth in the judge's opinion,

> most of the remaining 40% [of the information used by Franklin to create the maps in question as 60% had been created using maps from the United States Geological Survey and the Delaware Valley Regional Planning Commission] was from information taken from ADC [Alexendria Drafting] atlases.

Nevertheless, the judge ruled that while Franklin Maps did copy from a copyrightable publication, the amount copied was too minimal to support a claim of infringement and because Franklin Maps "generally copied only unprotectible facts," it did not infringe upon Alexandria's copyrights.[16]

This issue often comes up in the context of surveying plats and site plans. For example, in *Sparaco v. Lawler*, a land surveyor sued defendants alleging

13 499 U.S. 340 (1991).

14 The court distinguished between "creating" and "discovering."

15 43 U.S.P.Q.2d (BNA) 1247 (E.D. Pa. 1997).

16 It is important to note that the parties subsequently entered into a settlement agreement which vacated the judgement.

that the defendants copied his site plan in violation of copyright law.[17] In this case Sparaco claimed copyright both in the existing features of the site and in his proposals for physical improvements. The court found that

> [t]o the extent that the site plan sets forth the existing physical characteristics of the site, including its shape and dimensions, the grade contours, and the location of existing elements, it sets forth facts; copyright does not bar the copying of such facts.

However, the court did find that there was sufficient creativity in the proposed physical improvements as to qualify for copyright protection.

As technology has evolved, courts have had to apply these principles to new fact patterns. For example, in *Darden v. Peters* the court ruled that the Copyright Office's denial of copyright registration for a series of maps that had been created by taking a digital Census map of the U.S. and simply changing the coloring, adding shading, and selecting a font to use in labelling of states was valid. The court states that these changes were not sufficiently creative to receive copyright protection.[18]

In *Niehues v. Whitemyer*, Whitemyer was alleged to have created posters from Nieheus' copyrighted ski trail maps without a license or permission.[19] In a court decision regarding summary judgment, the judge stated that

> for purposes of copyright protection, maps are considered pictorial, factual compilations, "presenting information about geographic relationships" of naturally occurring objects. The "[p]hysical facts such as the names of geographic locations, landmasses, bodies of water and landmarks are not capable of copyright protection." Basic maps featuring "color, shading, and labels that use standard fonts and shapes do not meet the minimum level of creativity for copyright protection." "The protection that each map receives extends only to its original expression, and neither the facts nor the idea embodied in the maps is protected." To determine whether a map contains protectable elements, courts look at "creativity in both the selection, coordination, and arrangement of the facts that they depict, and the pictorial way in which they are depicted."

The judge added that

> [d]rawing the line between the unprotected ideas or facts within a work, and the creator's original expression of the ideas or facts, is the most

17 303 F.3d 460 (2nd Cir 2002).
18 488 F.3d 277 (4th Cir. May 24, 2007).
19 *Niehues v. Whitemyer*, Case No. 1:21-cv-00134-DBB-CMR J (D. Utah, June 9, 2023) Retrieved May 16, 2024 from https://www.govinfo.gov/content/pkg/USCOURTS-utd-1_21-cv-00134/pdf/USCOURTS-utd-1_21-cv-00134-0.pdf

> complex part of the legal copying inquiry. Courts are instructed to take an ad hoc approach, evaluating works on a case-by-case basis, keeping in mind that the primary objective of copyright is 'not to reward the labor of authors but to promote the Progress of Science and useful Arts.

In finding that copyright had not been violated, the *Niehues* court held that

> [u]nder governing law, the factual, naturally occurring, geographic information portrayed in the Big Sky map is not protected by copyright. Only Mr. Niehues's creativity in his selection of facts, and artistic expression in depicting the natural, geographic features, is protectable. Yet Plaintiffs point to no record evidence identifying how the map meets the minimum level of creativity and artistic expression for copyright protection.

While from a strictly legal standpoint it makes sense that data does not receive the same level of copyright protection as other intangible property such as software, the distinction raises significant challenges for organizations that collect or produce geospatial information. For example, businesses might question whether to invest significant capital to generate and maintain geospatial information if there is a significant risk that another organization will simply copy it and begin using it. In addition, business models are moving from separate software and data licenses to "Software as a Service" (SaaS) and "Data as a Service" (DaaS) models. In cases where software and data are being licensed together, the lines could become increasingly blurred as to what is protected by copyright and what is not. As will be discussed in more detail later, this becomes even more challenging with generative artificial intelligence (AI), as the training data and models are often in a "black box" such that even the AI operators cannot say for sure how information was generated.

Legality of Web Scraping

Web scraping is the process of using software to extract information from websites. It is a common tool used by the geospatial community to collect data. However, it poses complex legal and ethical issues. For example, if the web scraping captures images, videos, music, or text, it may violate copyright law, unless it is considered "fair use." Unfortunately, the concept of fair use with respect to many web scraping applications is still evolving. For example, the New York Times sued OpenAI for copyright infringement, claiming that the company scraped articles for its popular ChatGPT AI system and that fair use did not apply.

Web scraping raises other legal issues. For example, the Terms of Service (ToS) for many websites explicitly prohibit web scraping. Violating these ToS may result in claims of damages under contract law. In addition, web scraping has been alleged to violate federal and state laws, such as the Computer Fraud and Abuse Act mentioned previously, particularly if the scraping involves creating fraudulent accounts in order to access the data.

The most important case regarding web scraping to date is *hiQ Labs, Inc. v. LinkedIn, Corp.*[20] LinkedIn brought a claim against hiQ for scraping data individuals had posted about themselves on LinkedIn's publicly available website. LinkedIn claimed that hiQ's unauthorized actions violated both the Computer Fraud and Abuse Act (CFAA and LinkedIn's Terms of Service (resulting in a breach of contract and an unfair competition claim). After a lengthy series of court cases, the U.S. Court of Appeals suggested that LinkedIn could prevail on claims associated with hiQ's violation of LinkedIn's Terms of Service. However, it chose not to overturn a lower court's ruling that unauthorized web scraping, by itself, did not violate the CFAA.[21]

Unfortunately, from a geospatial law standpoint at least, the parties settled the case shortly after the Court of Appeals decision, so a final decision was not made as to whether web scraping was a breach of LinkedIn's Terms of Service. However, the court's decision in *LinkedIn* regarding the applicability of CFAA to web scraping was subsequently used in the court's decision in *Meta Platforms v BrandTotal.*[22] In *BrandTotal* the court stated that when a website is made available to the public without any authentication requirement, the concept of "without authorization," a key component of the CFAA, does not apply. As a result, the court found that BrandTotal did not violate the CFAA by scraping Meta's websites.

Government Data

Another unique aspect is the important role of federal and state government agencies in the geospatial ecosystem as data providers. The federal government is precluded by law from seeking copyright protection from any work.[23] However, as will be discussed throughout this book, even if geospatial information created or generated by federal agencies is not subject to copyright protection, there may be other reasons why this information is not made publicly available. Often these issues arise in the context of requests for information under the Freedom of Information Act (FOIA).[24] The intent of FOIA is to promote transparency and facilitate public participation in the democratic process. As a result, federal agencies are required to disclose any requested records unless the records fall under one of nine exemptions. These

20 938 F.3d 985 (9th Cir. 2019).

21 The court did suggest that the use of contractors to create fraudulent accounts for the explicit purpose of collecting data, could be a violation of CFAA.

22 *Meta Platforms v BrandTotal,* 605 F. Supp. 3d 1218 (N.D. Cal. 2022).

23 17 U.S. Code § 105(a).

24 5 U.S.C. § 552.

exemptions, which are designed to balance public interest against potential harm are as follows:

1. Information that is classified to protect national security.
2. Information related solely to the internal personnel rules and practices of an agency.
3. Information that is prohibited from disclosure by another federal law.
4. Trade secrets or commercial or financial information that is confidential or privileged.
5. Certain privileged communications within or between agencies.
6. Information that, if disclosed, would invade another individual's personal privacy.
7. Certain information compiled for law enforcement.
8. Information that concerns the supervision of financial institutions.
9. Geological information on wells.

There have been several reported court cases in which government agencies have attempted to reject FOIA requests pertaining to geospatial information. Agencies have attempted to use several of the FOIA exemptions to avoid having to release geospatial information. The results have varied.

For example, in *DeLorme Publishing v. National Oceanic and Atmospheric Administration*, NOAA rejected a FOIA request for electronic raster compilations of its nautical charts.[25] NOAA successfully argued that since the charts had been created in anticipation of, and during, a Cooperative Research and Development Agreement (CRADA), the information was subject to the Federal Technology Transfer Act, which prohibited NOAA from disclosing that information for five years. Therefore, Exemption 3 of FOIA – prohibiting disclosure by another federal law – applied.

However, in *Milner v. Department of Navy*, an organization sought to obtain maps and data relating to the effects of Navy's explosion activities. The Navy rejected the request under Exemption 2 regarding information pertaining solely to internal personnel rules and practices.[26] However, the Supreme Court rejected this argument and required the information to be released. Similarly, in *Audubon Society v. US Forest Service*, the Maricopa County Audubon Society made a FOIA request of the U.S. Forest Service, seeking maps that would identify Mexican spotted owl nests sites.[27] The Forest Service rejected the request on the grounds that the maps were "management territory maps" and therefore "related solely to the internal personnel

25 *DeLorme Publishing v. National Oceanic and Atmospheric Administration*, 917 F. Supp 867 (D. Maine March 12, 1996).
26 *Milner v. Department of Navy*, 562 U.S. 562 (March 7, 2011).
27 *Audubon Society v. US Forest Service*, 104 F.3d 1201 (10th Cir. 1997).

rules and practices" of the agency. The court rejected that argument and required the disclosure of the maps.

Unlike the federal government, some states and localities do claim copyright in their data, including geospatial information. For example, in *Seago v. Horry*, the Horris County GIS department developed a digital database that combined several layers of information onto one digital map of the county.[28] This process involved aerial images, various types of data, and a unique process to continually update the maps. The county applied copyright protection on certain data layers. A company that collected electronic mapping data from government entities across the state to then provide access to paying customers made a request under the state's FOIA law for copies of the county's orthophoto and GIS data. The company agreed to pay a fee for the data; however it refused to sign a licensing agreement that acknowledged Horry County's copyright on the information and restricted further commercial use of the information. The Supreme Court of South Carolina found South Carolina law allowed Horry County to claim copyright in the county's GIS data which had been specially created. The court also found that while the county had to comply with the FOIA request, it could restrict subsequent commercial use by the recipient. Similarly, in *County of Suffolk v. First American Real Estate Solutions*, the Second Circuit court found that Suffolk County could hold copyright in its tax maps and that the state's FOIA did not preclude the county from enforcing the associated rights.[29]

Several states have laws in place that preclude or limit copyright protection for state and local data. For example, in *Microdecisions v. Skinner*, under similar facts as *Seago vs. Horry*, the court found that under Florida law, the county property appraiser could not require prospective commercial users of the GIS maps obtained under the state's Freedom of Information law to first enter into a licensing agreement.[30] Specifically, the court held that "the fact that a person seeking access to public records wishes to use them in a commercial enterprise does not alter his or her rights under Florida's public records law." The court added that if the Florida legislature wanted to preclude such access to GIS maps, it could exempt such disclosures. Similarly, in *Greenwich v. Whitaker*, the Supreme Court of Connecticut held that city GIS data was not a "trade secret" and therefore could be disclosed.[31]

A slightly different issue was addressed in *Pictometry International v. Freedom of Information*.[32] The issue in this case was the applicability of the state's FOIA to proprietary geospatial information that the government agency had purchased from a commercial vendor. The case concerned an FOIA request that the plaintiff had made for copies of oblique aerial images

28 *Seago v. Horry*, 378 S.C. 414, (June 26. 2008).
29 261 F.3rd 179 (2nd Cir. 2001).
30 889 So. 2d 871 (2nd D. Fl, 2004).
31 (874 A.2d 785, June 21, 2005).
32 59 A3d 172 (Conn: Supreme Court 2013).

that the Town of Greenwich had purchased. The Town of Greenwich claimed that the "federal law" exemption to the state FOIA law applied because the images were protected by federal copyright. The Connecticut Supreme Court overruled the decisions of a lower court and held that information copyrighted by a third party was not subject to disclosure under the state's FOIA.[33]

Artificial Intelligence

The geospatial community has been a significant user of artificial intelligence ((AI) for many years. However, the broader business community – and by implication the legal and regulatory community – have only just recently begun to realize the potential of this powerful technology. As noted previously, generative AI is raising significant concerns regarding violating copyright when creating training data. However, there is also an issue regarding when the output from an AI system can be protected by copyright. In one of the first cases on this matter, the United States District Court for the District of Columbia granted the United States Copyright Office a summary judgment that copyright on artwork generated by an AI model owned by the plaintiff was not subject to copyright protection.[34] The plaintiff asserted that since he owned the AI model, the artwork generated was a "work-for-hire" and that he should be granted copyright protection in the work. However, the court agreed with the USPTO that a work created absent any human involvement is not copyrightable. This was in keeping with guidance issued by the Copyright Office in March 2023.[35] The court did note that it is still an open question as to what level of human involvement is required to make a work copyrightable.

This decision was similar to other decisions pertaining to the importance of human involvement in creative works. For example, there was an infamous dispute regarding a photographer trying to assert copyright over "selfies" that a monkey had taken of itself. According to the photographer, he had set up a tripod, framed the image and the exposure, and had simply given the monkey a button to push to capture the image. However, while the dispute was playing out, the U.S. Copyright Office published guidance clearly stating that a photograph taken by a monkey is a work that lacks human authorship.[36] (Of note, a court subsequently decided that the monkey could not claim copyright in the image.)[37]

33 Of note, the 2005 Defence Authorization Act exempted commercial satellite imagery from the federal FOIA law.

34 See e.g. Kasunic, R. (2023). *Letter to Lindberg, V.* Retrieved December 12, 2023, from www.copyright.gov/docs/zarya-of-the-dawn.pdf.

35 U.S. Copyright Office. (2021). *Compendium of U.S. Copyright office practices §306* (3rd ed.), U.S. Copyright Office.

36 See e.g., Monkey Selfie Copyright Dispute. (n.d.). *In Wikipedia.* Retrieved December 14, 2023, from https://en.wikipedia.org/wiki/Monkey_selfie_copyright_dispute.

37 Kravets, D. (2016, January 6). Judge says monkey cannot own copyright to famous selfies. *Ars Technica.* Retrieved December 12, 2023, from https://arstechnica.com/tech-policy/2016/01/judge-says-monkey-cannot-own-copyright-to-famous-selfies/.

Multiple Datasets in a Single Product or Service

The power of geospatial information lies in its ability to aggregate it with a variety of other datasets. However, in doing so, one must consider the intellectual property rights associated with the wide range of data sources: commercial products, federal agencies, and state and local government. When creating products and services by aggregating geospatial information from different sources, it is important to understand whether each dataset is subject to copyright and the terms of the associated license and/or data sharing agreement with respect to rights in the newly created derivative product.

International Considerations

While this textbook focuses on U.S. law, the geospatial ecosystem is inherently international. As a result, geospatial professionals should not assume that the legal protections offered to intellectual property in the U.S. apply in other countries. It is often necessary to consider intellectual property rights from an international perspective. For example, the European Union's Database Law grants greater protection to databases than provided in the U.S.[38]

Conclusion

As this chapter has detailed, it is important for geospatial professionals to understand intellectual property rights in geospatial technology and information. Geospatial professionals should also consider adopting best practices to both ensure that their intellectual property is adequately protected and to make sure they do not inadvertently violate the intellectual property rights of third parties. These best practices include

- identifying and documenting an organization's intellectual property
- implementing measures to secure intellectual property
- obtaining proper permissions before using or accessing intellectual property belonging to others
- including adequate protections of intellectual property rights in agreements with customers, vendors, and partners and complying with applicable terms
- using appropriate notices and disclosure, such as copyright notices or trademark symbols
- monitoring intellectual property for unauthorized use by third parties and enforcing rights when necessary

38 Directive 96/9/EC of the European Parliament and of the Council of 11 March 1996 on the legal protection of databases.

3 Location Privacy[1]

Introduction

This chapter will discuss the existing legal and policy framework for location privacy in the U.S. It will begin by introducing the foundational principles of privacy law. It will then explain how the legal framework for federal government agencies on matters pertaining to privacy differs from those of the private sector. This will include a discussion of how the concept of "a reasonable expectation of privacy" under the Fourth Amendment from a location standpoint is evolving. The chapter will then provide an overview of the growing number of legal requirements imposed upon businesses to protect geospatial information that they obtain about individuals. It will conclude with a discussion of where privacy law is going and its likely impact on the geospatial community as it adopts new technologies, collects new data types, and develops novel applications.

There are several important considerations reading this chapter:

- First, privacy is the word that is often used to describe society's concerns when a new technology is introduced. These concerns are often characterized as a privacy issue when in many cases people simply do not understand a new technology, and this makes them feel uncomfortable. This is not a new phenomenon. For example, similar issues were raised when the first commercial camera was introduced in the late 1800s.[2] The growing number of low-cost sensors and platforms that collect geospatial information (many of which can be associated with an individual), improvements in technology that make it easier to store and transmit data cheaply and more efficiently, and powerful tools, such as artificial intelligence (AI),

1 This chapter will refer to privacy law because that is often how the term is used in the United States. However, in many parts of the world, the concept has become less about privacy, which as we will see can be difficult to define, to data protection. The concept of data protection instead of privacy is becoming increasingly common in the U.S. as well.

2 See e.g., Burrows, L. (2013, July 24). To be let alone: Brandeis foresaw privacy problems. *BrandeisNOW*. Retrieved December 12, 2023, from www.brandeis.edu/now/2013/july/privacy.html.

DOI: 10.4324/9781003329961-3

have all contributed to the privacy concerns associated with location information.

- Second, privacy law generally involves a balancing of several different, but important, interests. For example, lawmakers and regulators often must balance the perceived privacy risks for individuals with the value to the public of the geospatial information being collected or used by government agencies. For example, after the terrorist acts on September 11, 2001, many Americans were less concerned about privacy than they were about making sure that there was not another attack on U.S. soil. However, after those concerns became less acute, greater attention was paid to the information – including geospatial information – that the U.S. government was collecting on U.S. citizens to combat terrorism.
- Another important consideration is who will be the ultimate decision-maker as to whether an individual's privacy has been violated: legislators, regulators, the courts, industry? Each will bring different levels of expertise and perspective with respect to geospatial information and the associated risks. In the coming years, aspects of privacy law pertaining to geospatial information are likely to be based upon actions of all four, and the differences among them could have significant impacts on the geospatial ecosystem in the U.S.

Fundamentals of Privacy Law

Historically, privacy law in the United States, and around the globe, has developed based upon the Fair Information Practice Principles (FIPPs). The FIPPs were introduced in the 1970s to address concerns associated with broad use of computers. The primary elements of the FIPPs are as follows[3]:

1. *Collection Limitation Principle* – There should be limits to the collection of personal information, and any such information should be obtained by lawful and fair means and, where appropriate, with the knowledge or consent of the data subject.
2. *Data Quality Principle* – Personal information should be relevant to the purposes for which they are to be used and should be accurate, complete, and kept up to date to the extent necessary for such purposes.
3. *Purpose Specification Principle* – The purposes for which personal information are collected should be specified no later than at the time of data collection, and subsequent use should be limited to the fulfilment of those purposes.

3 OECD. (n.d.). *Recommendation of the council concerning guidelines governing the protection of privacy and transborder flows of personal information*. Retrieved December 10, 2023, from https://legalinstruments.oecd.org/en/instruments/OECD-LEGAL-0188.

4. *Use Limitation Principle* – Personal information should not be disclosed, made available, or otherwise used for purposes other than those specified except with the consent of the data subject or as required by law.
5. *Security Safeguards Principle* – Personal information should be protected by reasonable security safeguards.
6. *Openness Principle* – An organization should have a general policy of openness about developments, practices, and policies with respect to the personal information it collects and uses.
7. *Individual Participation Principle* – Individuals should have the right to obtain confirmation of whether an organization has personal information relating to them.
8. *Accountability Principle* – An organization should be accountable for complying with the FIPP principles.

Technology has evolved since the introduction of the FIPPs, resulting in significant changes in (i) what personal information is collected and (ii) how it is collected, used, and shared. However, these general principles are still the foundations for privacy law in the U.S (and around the world). For example, major federal laws, such as the Health Insurance Portability and Accountability Act (HIPAA), Gramm-Leach-Bliley Act (GLB), and the Family Educational Rights and Privacy Act (FERPA), as well as comprehensive state privacy laws, are all based upon these principles. The challenge, as this chapter will discuss, is applying these principles to geospatial information.

It is also important to note that the scope of personal information that is protected in the U.S. is broadening and increasingly covering subsets of geospatial information. Initially, privacy concerns were limited to what was known as "personally identifiable information" or PII. As the name suggests, PII was limited to information that could be used to identify a person, either directly or in combination with other information, such as their social security number, driver's license, or credit card information. For example, all states have data breach laws that require a business to notify customers if there has been a data security incident of a certain threshold resulting in the loss of PII.

However, the laws concerning privacy have expanded the definition of protected information. For example, the California Consumer Privacy Act (CCPA) protects "any information that identifies, relates to, describes, is capable of being associated with, or could reasonably be linked, directly or indirectly, with a particular consumer or household."[4] The reader will recognize that geospatial information is such a powerful tool that many types of geospatial information could be associated with a consumer or household.

4 California Consumer Privacy Act, Cal. Civil Code § 1798.100 et seq. (2018).

Why Developing Laws to Protect Location Privacy is Difficult

Despite growing efforts to address the privacy concerns associated with geospatial information, there are several reasons why protecting location privacy will be a challenge. One of the most difficult aspects will be defining what type of information is being protected as it is much more difficult to define geospatial information pertaining to an individual (e.g., location privacy) than it is to define other types of personal information (i.e., health records, social security numbers, driver license numbers, etc.). For example, the CCPA, as amended, protects "data that is derived from a device and that is used or intended to be used to locate a consumer within a geographic area that is equal to or less than the area of a circle with a radius of one thousand, eight hundred and fifty (1,850) feet, except as prescribed by regulations."[5] The Federal Trade Commission has issued a rule that includes a definition of geolocation data under the Children's Online Privacy Protection Act (COPPA) as "geolocation information sufficient to identify street name and name of a city or town."[6] Under the Virginia Consumer Data Protection Act, protected location information is "information derived from technology, including but not limited to global positioning system level latitude and longitude coordinates or other mechanisms, that directly identifies the specific location of a natural person with precision and accuracy within a radius of 1,750 feet."[7] (The content of communications or any data generated by or connected to advanced utility metering infrastructure systems or equipment for use by a utility is excluded.[8]) On the other hand, Colorado law protects "an individual who can be readily identified, directly or indirectly, in particular by reference to an identifier such as a name, an identification number, *specific geolocation data* or online identifier"[9] [emphasis added], but the geolocation data to be protected is not defined. These differences are significant for organizations with operations across the U.S. trying to determine if and how to comply.

There is often a temporal component to location privacy that is less relevant to other types of personal information. For example, a person's social security number is sensitive for their entire life (and beyond). The privacy concerns associated with knowing an individual's location in the present are much different than knowing where a person was last week or two years ago. The former raises a concern over safety, while the concerns of the latter are more related to patterns of life. Both raise privacy issues, but the risks – and by consequence the mitigation measures – are very different.

There are also cultural, gender, age, religious, and social components to location privacy. While almost everyone will agree that financial and medical

5 California Civil Code, Section 1798.140.
6 16 C.F.R. Part 312.
7 Va Code: § 59.1–575.
8 Id.
9 Colorado Privacy Act (§6–1–1301 to §6–1–1313).

records are sensitive and should be protected, cultural factors result in individuals having a different sense of location privacy concerns. This makes it challenging to develop effective laws and policies.

Location information also can be collected in many more ways than other types of personal information. For example, a person's location can be inferred from their mobile device, an IP address, key cards used to enter an office building, and records of ATM and credit card transactions.

Alternatively, it could be collected by a CCTV camera, a license plate reader, sensors mounted on drones, aircraft, and possibly in the future, satellites. Each of these technologies and applications are regulated by different government agencies, which will likely lead to different requirements. As geospatial products and services are developed by combining data from a variety of sensors, the complexity in complying with these differing requirements could be significant.

Another consideration is that unlike most other types of personal information, a person discloses their location every time they go out and visit a store, drive to the doctors, or attend a church service. Therefore, treating this information with the same level of care as a credit card number, a driver's license number, medical history, or sexual orientation raises complex issues.

Historically, courts have found that a person loses his or her expectation of privacy when going out in public. For example, the Supreme Court has ruled on Fourth Amendment privacy issues that citizens do not have a reasonable expectation of privacy while in public. However, as will be discussed in more detail later in this chapter, this legal concept is evolving.

Many privacy laws have exceptions for data that is publicly available. In Colorado, the regulations provide that businesses do not need to protect information that has been made available to the public. With respect to location information, the regulations provide that a visual observation of an individual's physical presence in a public place by another person is not protected, but including data collected by a device in the individual's possession is protected.[10] Courts in other jurisdictions will have to decide how that principle of publicly available applies to the disclosure of an individual's location in public.

For example, in the case of *Boring v. Google*,[11] the Borings claimed that Google violated several aspects of their privacy by coming onto their property to take images that were subsequently posted on Google Street View.[12] They sought $25,000 in damages. In ruling against the Borings, the court found that "[n]o person of ordinary sensibilities would be shamed, humiliated, or

10 Colorado Privacy Act Rules 4 CCR 904-3 Rule 2.02.

11 3d Cir. Pa. Jan. 28, 2010.

12 The claims under Pennsylvania law were "Intrusion Upon Seclusion" and "Publicity Given to Private Life."

have suffered mentally as a result of a vehicle entering into his or her ungated driveway and photographing the view from there." It also noted,

> Though not pertinent to our decision, we note Google's assertion, which is not seriously contested by the Borings, that the Street View photograph is similar to a view of the Borings' house that was once publicly available online through the County Assessor's website.[13]

It is also important to note that geospatial information is much more versatile than other types of personal information. A person's location can be used to provide him or her critical governmental, societal, and business services. For example, emergency services can use a person's location to notify them of a forest fire. Similarly, location information can be used to find a lost child or a broken down or stolen car. The number and value of these services are increasing on an almost daily basis. Attempts to regulate the collection of location information could have a number of unintended consequences, such as making it more difficult to respond to a future pandemic.

Adding to the challenge of protecting location privacy is the number of potential privacy risks that must be considered from a location standpoint. These include the following:

- *Surveillance*: Unauthorized tracking of individuals by governments, corporations, or other third parties can violate privacy rights and lead to discrimination, exploitation, or other negative outcomes.
- *Profiling*: Companies can use location information to create profiles of individuals, which can be used for purposes such as credit scoring, employment decisions, and insurance underwriting.
- *Misuse*: Location information data can be misused for purposes such as stalking, harassment, or discrimination.
- *Errors*: Errors in location accuracy or precision can lead to wrongful arrest or cause other consequences.

As these risks vary, it will be challenging to develop comprehensive privacy laws that adequately address each.

Laws Impacting Collection and Use of Location Information

As the legal requirements concerning location privacy vary depending upon whether an organization is a government agency or whether it is a business, this book will discuss each separately.

13 *Id.*

Privacy Law and Government Agencies

Privacy Act of 1974

At the federal level, the Privacy Act of 1974 (the "Privacy Act") is the principal law governing the collection, maintenance, use, and dissemination of personal information by the federal government. It protects records of citizens in possession of the government and prevents unauthorized disclosure except for a limited list of exceptions.[14] A record is defined as

> any item, collection, or grouping of information about an individual that is maintained by an agency, including, but not limited to, his education, financial transactions, medical history, and criminal or employment history and that contains his name, or the identifying number, symbol, or other identifying particular assigned to the individual, such as a finger or voice print or a photograph.[15]

The Privacy Act sets forth a number of provisions that federal agencies must follow with respect to such records. These include (i) requiring agencies to provide notice when gathering and handling personal information; (ii) requiring government agencies to show an individual any records kept on him or her; and (iii) imposing restrictions on how agencies can share an individual's data with other people and agencies.

Given how long ago the Privacy Act was enacted, it should not be surprising to learn that it did not address in any meaningful way the collection, use, or sharing of citizens' location information. However, recently there have been other federal laws and policies pertaining to the federal government's collection and use of geospatial information that have highlighted the privacy issues associated with geolocation information. For example, the Geospatial Data Act of 2018 directs government agencies responsible for managing data for the U.S. national spatial data infrastructure to protect the privacy of citizens.[16] Furthermore, the National Institute of Standards and Technology (NIST) policy on de-identifying government datasets references the Geospatial Data Act of 2018 as a law that "significantly increased the need for expertise regarding privacy-preserving data analysis and data publishing techniques, such as de-identification."[17]

14 5 U.S.C. § 552a.
15 5 U.S.C. § 552a(a)(4).
16 743 U.S.C. Ch. 46 § 2808(a)(9).
17 National Institute of Standards and Technology. (2023). De-Identifying Government Datasets: Techniques and Governance (NIST SP 800–188). NIST Special Publication.

Freedom of Information Act

As noted in Chapter 2, the Freedom of Information Act balances a citizen's right to understand the government's operations with the government's obligation to protect sensitive information.

One of the FOIA exemptions is privacy. From a geospatial information standpoint, a question that arises is whether the aggregation of location-enabled datasets that do not otherwise contain PII that would be subject to the Privacy Act can encroach upon privacy interests such as to qualify under FOIA privacy exemption for disclosure. Unfortunately for geospatial practitioners, there is no simple answer to when location data is protected from disclosure under the FOIA. Rather, it requires a very fact-specific analysis. For example, in *Forest Guardians v. United States Federal Emergency Management Agency*, a conservation group was looking for electronic mapping files that showed the locations of structures insured under the Federal Emergency Management Agency (FEMA)'s National Insurance Flood Program.[18] The electronic map files did not include names and addresses, but the court found that FEMA did not have to disclose the requested information because there was no public interest in the disclosure, but if the information was disclosed, it could be used to determine the names and addresses of the homeowners. Those individuals might then be subject to unwanted solicitation from insurance companies, etc., that would violate their privacy.

However, in *News-Press v. U.S. Department of Homeland Security*, the court found that the disclosure by FEMA of addresses (without names) that received post-hurricane assistance was permitted.[19] The court found that there was substantial public interest in the information being released and that FEMA did not establish that such disclosure would constitute "a clearly unwarranted invasion of privacy." Similarly, in *Multi-Media Ag. v Department of Agriculture*, Multi-Media made an FOIA request for GIS information on farms that were receiving subsidies from the Department of Agriculture. No names and addresses were to be included in the request.[20] In balancing the public value of the information being released versus the privacy interest of the farmers, the court found that there was a substantial privacy interest in protecting the data on the farms as the livestock and crops were financial assets, and someone could conceivably use this information to determine an individual's financial situation. However, the court ultimately ruled that the benefit to the public in disclosing the information was greater than the privacy risks and therefore required the disclosure.[21]

18 410 F.3d 1214 (10th Cir. 2005).

19 489 F.3d 1173 (11th. 2007).

20 515 F.3d 1224, (D.C. Cir. 2008).

21 It is important to note however that in future legislation prohibited USDA from disclosure of certain geospatial information related to agricultural operations.

Other Federal Laws and Policies

As noted previously, there are a number of other laws and policies that restrict the ability of government agencies to collect or share personal information that has a location component. These include the Geospatial Data Act of 2018. The U.S. Census Bureau collects a large amount of information, including geospatial information, when conducting the decennial census. However, it is restricted from sharing this information, even with other government agencies, other than in statistical form by Title 13 Section 9 of the U.S. Code. As noted in a 2019 report by the Brennan Centre, the U.S. Department of Justice's Office of Legal Counsel has repeatedly found that the Census Act's confidentiality provisions take precedence over other laws that otherwise allow for the disclosure of personal information.[22]

In addition, government agencies have published guidance on privacy issues for technologies that are inherently geospatial or have a significant geospatial component. For example, in 2014 the Department of Energy issued a draft voluntary code of conduct on the development and deployment of smart grid technologies. It contained provisions regarding anonymizing personal data from a location standpoint.[23] Similarly, the National Highway Traffic Safety Administration (NHTSA) has published a "Federal Automated Vehicles Policy" that includes guidance on privacy, security, and data sharing in the development and deployment of autonomous vehicles (AVs).[24]

Fourth Amendment Issues

The Fourth Amendment of the U.S. Constitution is an important source of privacy protection in the United States. It provides that "[t]he right of the people to be secure in their persons, houses, papers, and effects, against unreasonable searches and seizures, shall not be violated."[25] *U.S. v. Katz*[26] is the seminal case in which Fourth Amendment protections were found to have created a right to privacy. The issue in *Katz* concerned a phone call Katz had placed from a public phone booth. Law enforcement had intercepted the call without first obtaining a warrant. The government argued that it was not

22 Percival, K. (2019, February 20). *Federal laws that protect census confidentiality*. Retrieved December 26, 2023, from www.brennancenter.org/our-work/research-reports/federal-laws-protect-census-confidentiality.

23 U.S. Department of Energy. (n.d.). *Data privacy and the smart grid: A Voluntary Code of Conduct (VCC) draft for public comment*. Retrieved December 31, 2023, from www.energy.gov/oe/articles/data-privacy-and-smart-grid-voluntary-code-conduct-vcc-draft-public-comment-september.

24 U.S. Department of Transportation. (n.d.). *AV Policy Guidance*. Retrieved December 31, 2023, from www.transportation.gov/sites/dot.gov/files/docs/AV%20policy%20guidance%20PDF.pdf.

25 U.S. Constitution (Amendment XIV).

26 389 U.S. 347 (1967).

required to obtain a warrant because the call was made from a public location, and therefore Katz had no expectation of privacy with respect to the call. However, the court found that by entering the telephone booth and closing its door, Katz had a reasonable expectation that the conversation would not be heard. Therefore, the government needed to obtain a warrant before tapping phone lines to listen in on the call.

Justice Harland's concurrent opinion in *Katz* set forth what has come to be known as the "reasonable expectation of privacy" test.[27] The test consists of two prongs. First, a court must determine whether an individual has exhibited an expectation of privacy. In the *Katz* case, this might include taking the call in a phone booth and closing the door. This is the objective component of the test.

Second, a court assesses whether society is prepared to recognize such an expectation of privacy as reasonable. For example, whispering in a crowded room so as not to be overheard might not be considered reasonable. This is the subjective component. Unless both tests are satisfied, a citizen does not have a reasonable expectation of privacy from a government search. As a result, the government (typically, but not always, law enforcement) is not required to obtain a warrant from a court.

The reasonable expectation of privacy test is used in many different contexts. From a geospatial law standpoint, the issue generally arises in two types of cases: remote sensing and tracking. Remote sensing cases involve law enforcement's use of remote sensing technology in public spaces. Tracking cases refers to the use of technology by law enforcement to track an individual's movements in public. Each will be discussed separately.

Remote Sensing Cases

In 1986, the U.S. Supreme Court applied the reasonable expectation of privacy test in two seminal cases. In *Dow Chemical Co. v. US*,[28] the court found that the Environmental Protection Agency (EPA) did not violate the Fourth Amendment rights of Dow Chemical when it used a plane to obtain aerial photographs to inspect the company's property without first obtaining a warrant. Similarly, in *California v. Ciraolo*,[29] the Supreme Court found that using data obtained from a plane hired by the police to overfly a suspect's home without obtaining a warrant in court did not violate the defendant's Fourth Amendment rights. The court stated in *Ciraolo* that "[i]n an age where private and commercial flight in the public airway is routine, it is unreasonable for respondent to expect that his marijuana plants were constitutionally

27 389 Id at 361.
28 476 U.S. 227 (1986).
29 476 U.S. 207 (1986).

protected from being observed by the naked eye."[30] The court affirmed this right three years later, in *Florida v. Riley*,[31] holding that police did not need to obtain a warrant to fly a helicopter over a home to collect images.

However, the courts set limitations on the government's right to collect remote sensing data. For example, the Supreme Court in *Kyllo v. U.S.*[32] found that the use of a thermal imaging device aimed at a private home without a warrant violated the individual's right to privacy. Specifically, the Court stated, "[w]here, as here, the Government uses a device that is not in general public use, to explore details of the home that would previously have been unknowable without physical intrusion, the surveillance is a 'search'; and is presumptively unreasonable with a warrant."[50]

Recently, there has been an increase of remote sensing cases, likely due to advancements in technology. In some cases the courts have begun to reverse some of the earlier decisions regarding reasonable expectations of privacy. For example, in 2015, the New Mexico Supreme Court ruled that a warrantless aerial surveillance over a defendant's yard was unconstitutional under the New Mexico Constitution.[33] Specifically, the court, which overruled a lower court's findings, stated that "prolonged hovering close enough to the ground to cause interference with Davis' property transformed this surveillance from a lawful observation of an area left open to public view to an unconstitutional intrusion into Davis' expectation of privacy."

Courts have reached conflicting conclusions as to whether mounting a sensor on a pole continuously monitoring a suspect's house requires a warrant.[34] Several federal courts have concluded that police can use pole cameras to surveil homes without any constitutional limit. In contrast, the U.S. Court of Appeals for the Fifth Circuit and several state courts have ruled that long-term pole-camera surveillance of a home is a Fourth Amendment search, for which a warrant is required.

Given the proliferation of remote sensing technology, one can expect an increase in cases that will test the limit of what society considers reasonable. For example, the Supreme Court has not addressed whether an individual's expectation of privacy from an image taken from a satellite – as compared to aerial imagery – would be different. However, given the capabilities of commercial satellites to collect very high quality electro-optical imagery, courts soon may be asked to address this issue. In addition, commercial satellites are being deployed with sensors that collect a wide range of phenomenologies,

30 *Id* at 215.
31 488 U.S. 445 (1979).
32 533 U.S. 27 (2001).
33 *State v. Davis*, 263 P. 3d 953, 961 (N.M. Ct. App. 2011.
34 See e.g. American Civil Liberties Union. (2023). Warrantless pole-camera surveillance by police is dangerous. *The Supreme Court Can Stop It.* Retrieved December 31, 2023, from www.aclu.org/news/privacy-technology/warrantless-pole-camera-surveillance-by-police-is-dangerous-the-supreme-court-can-stop-it.

such as radar, thermal infrared, and hyperspectral data. Could these new sensors detect signatures that could be used to identify a potential illicit activity, and if so, what are the privacy implications?

Tracking

There has also been an increase in tracking cases. Historically, courts have found that law enforcement's use of technology to track an individual's movements in public was permitted under the Constitution. One of the seminal tracking cases was *United States v. Knott*. In *Knott*, the court found that the police's placing of a radio transmitter inside chemical containers without obtaining a warrant in order to track a suspect's movements did not violate the defendant's Fourth Amendment rights. Similarly, in *U.S. v. Garcia*, 474 F.3d 994 (7th Cir. 2007) the court found that law enforcement's use of GPS devise on car without a warrant was permitted.

Many tracking cases involve the government's efforts to obtain cell tower location information (CTLI) from telecommunication companies that are collected in connection with providing mobile phone services. Traditionally, courts had found that law enforcement did not need a warrant to obtain location information from telecommunication companies.

However, the concept of location privacy in the United States is beginning to evolve, in part due to changes in technology. It is increasingly easier to use geospatial technology to continuously monitor an individual's movements, even without using a tracking device. One would expect under the "reasonable expectation of privacy" test that given the increased ease to collection location, expectations for privacy should decrease. However, the reverse is happening: the courts appear to be expanding what is considered a reasonable expectation for privacy.

The beginning of this change can be found in the decision of the Supreme Court in *U.S. v. Jones*.[35] The Supreme Court was asked to decide whether law enforcement was required to obtain a warrant before using a tracking device to monitor an individual's movements in public. The court found that the act of placing a device on an automobile without a warrant was a violation of the suspect's Fourth Amendment rights under what may be considered to be an archaic theory of trespass. However, in the concurring and dissenting opinions, a majority of the justices appear to suggest that long-term tracking taking place in public violated the Fourth Amendment. This concept, generally referred to as the "mosaic theory" suggests that if the government collects enough information about an individual over time, it infringes that individual's privacy expectation.

This issue was addressed in more detail in the U.S. Supreme Court case *U.S. v Carpenter*.[36] The Court held that the government violated the Fourth

35 132 S. Ct. 945 (2012).
36 138 S. Ct. 2206 (2018).

Amendment by accessing historical records containing the physical locations of cell phones without a search warrant. In not obtaining a warrant, law enforcement had relied upon what is known as the "third-party doctrine" exemption – which provides that a person has no legitimate expectation of privacy in information it voluntary turns over to a third party. Finding that the government had constitutionally violated Mr. Carpenter's reasonable expectation of privacy by acquiring this private information without a warrant, the court ruled that concerns over location information supersedes third party doctrine and that an individual has a legitimate expectation of privacy, from a Fourth Amendment perspective, in the record of physical movements captured through cell-site location information.

A 2021 case, *Leaders of a Beautiful Struggle, et al. v. Baltimore Police Department*, is an example of both a remote sensing and a tracking case. In *Beautiful Struggle*, the Fourth Circuit Court of Appeals held that an aerial surveillance program operated by Baltimore's police department violated the Fourth Amendment. The program involved the warrantless tracking of people on city streets through aerial surveillance. Even though the surveillance was of activities in public, the court found, relying in part on Carpenter, that under the Fourth Amendment people have a reasonable expectation of privacy that their outdoor movements are not being tracked for long period of times by the government.

As noted throughout this book, one of the challenges of location privacy standpoint is that many technologies can be used to determine – or at least infer – an individual's location. Each raises issues of what should be considered a reasonable expectation of privacy. For example, technology that spoofs a cell phone tower to obtain the location of a suspect's mobile device, known as "stingray technology" had been used by law enforcement for a number of years. However, beginning in the late 2010's, courts began to rule that the use of such devices without a warrant violated an individual's Fourth Amendment rights.[37] Subsequently, both the Department of Justice and the Department of Homeland Security announced that they had updated their policies to require a warrant before using stingray technology in most circumstances.[38] However, the technology is still being used, and the courts are still struggling to address the complicated privacy issues.[39]

37 See e.g., Engadget. (2017). *Court rules stingray use without a warrant violates fourth amendment*. Retrieved December 31, 2023, from www.engadget.com/2017-09-21-court-stingray-without-warrant-violates-fourth-amendment.html.

38 See e.g., The Verge. (2015). *Homeland security will now get warrants for stingray surveillance*. Retrieved December 31, 2023, from www.theverge.com/2015/10/21/9583438/homeland-security-stingray-warrants-phone-tracking.

39 Criminal Legal News. (2020). *Fourth circuit requests further information on stingray device to determine whether it violates fourth amendment rights*. Retrieved December 31, 2023, from www.criminallegalnews.org/news/2020/jul/15/fourth-circuit-requests-further-information-stingray-device-determine-whether-it-violates-fourth-amendment-rights/.

Courts are also trying to determine the Fourth Amendment issues associated with "geofence warrants." A geofence warrant is issued by a judge and compels companies that collect location information on customers to provide location data for all devices during a specified time and within a specified geographic area. They are much broader than traditional search warrants as they can include information from individuals that are not suspects. This raises significant privacy concerns. For example, in *People v. Dawes* the court refused to allow evidence obtained from a geofence warrant. Specifically, it found that a search warrant was required under the California Electronic Communications Privacy Act and that the geographic area covered by the warrant was overly broad for purposes of the Fourth Amendment.[40]

Privacy Law and Businesses

Federal Trade Commission

Unlike many other countries, there is no comprehensive federal privacy or data protection law in the United States.[41] Instead, the U.S. data protection framework at the federal level consists primarily of sector-specific laws. For example, the Health Insurance Portability and Accountability Act (HIPAA) protects health records, Gramm-Leach-Bliley Act (GLB) protects financial records, and Family Educational Rights and Privacy Act (FERPA) protects records containing personal information. None of these deal with location privacy, although as previously noted location information is covered under the Children's Online Privacy Protection Act (COPPA).

There are various other privacy initiatives at the federal level that will impact geospatial information. For over a decade, bills have been introduced in Congress that would regulate location information. Some of these have specifically targeted location information, such as the Geolocation Privacy and Surveillance Act, commonly known as the "GPS Act." First introduced by Senator Ron Wyden and Representative Jason Chaffetz in 2011, the GPS Act sought to establish a legal framework for how government agencies and the private sector could collect and use location information. It was reintroduced in 2017 but has never become law. Others are bills for comprehensive privacy laws that protect certain types of location information. These too have not become law, although the patchwork of state privacy laws, discussed in the next section, is putting pressure on Congress to pass a comprehensive federal law that would likely include location privacy.

40 See. National Association of Criminal Defense Lawyers. (n.d.). *Dawes order granting suppression*. Retrieved December 31, 2023, from www.nacdl.org/getattachment/9921c3b4-21bc-4471-b166-56731fe40aad/dawes-order-granting-suppression.pdf.

41 Although, as will be discussed later, there have been a number of bills introduced in Congress to address this topic.

Within the Executive Branch, one of the primary missions of the Federal Trade Commission ("FTC") is consumer protection. Section 5 of the Federal Trade Commission Act grants the FTC broad enforcement authority to protect consumers from unfair trade practices. Initially, the FTC used this enforcement authority with respect to privacy to ensure that businesses complied with the privacy statements posted on their websites. The FTC then began to take enforcement actions against companies that lost (or had stolen) their customers' sensitive personal information, even if such loss did not violate a stated privacy policy with respect to such data. Enforcement actions included both fines and other civil penalties.

Eventually, the FTC began to initiate enforcement actions against companies that were collecting personal information, including location information, without proper notice to and consent from consumers. For example, in 2015, Nomi Technologies Inc., a retail analytics company, agreed to settle charges brought by the FTC that it tracked consumers' movements through its in-store tracking technology without consumers' knowledge or consent. Similarly, in 2018, LocationSmart, a location data broker, agreed to settle charges that it sold consumers' real-time location data to third parties without consumers' knowledge or consent.

The FTC's most aggressive enforcement action with respect to location privacy occurred in 2022, when it brought an action against Kochava Inc, alleging Kochava was selling location data collected from consumers' mobile devices and from other data brokers to assist in advertising and analyzing foot traffic at stores or other locations.[42] The FTC's complaint included several examples of how consumers could be harmed. For example, it alleged the data could be used to identify consumers who have visited an abortion clinic and, as a result, may have had or contemplated having an abortion. The FTC also alleged in its complaint that the data could also be used to identify medical professionals who perform, or assist in the performance, of abortion services or to track consumers to places of worship and thus reveal the religious beliefs and practices of consumers.

In 2022, the FTC also published an advanced notice on proposed rulemaking (APRM), seeking public comment on the prevalence of commercial surveillance and data security practices that harm consumers.[43] The purpose of the APRM was to determine whether the FTC should implement new rules on the ways in which companies collect, aggregate, protect, use, analyze, and retain consumer data. The FTC was also trying to determine how to address

42 Federal Trade Commission. (n.d.). *FTC v Kochava, Inc.* Retrieved January 1, 2024, from www.ftc.gov/legal-library/browse/cases-proceedings/ftc-v-kochava-inc.

43 Federal Trade Commission. (2022). *FTC explores rules cracking down on commercial surveillance and lax data security practices.* Retrieved January 1, 2024, from www.ftc.gov/news-events/news/press-releases/2022/08/ftc-explores-rules-cracking-down-commercial-surveillance-lax-data-security-practices.

the transfer, sharing, selling, or other monetizing of data in ways that are unfair or deceptive.

Location information was one of the data types that the FTC expressed concern about in the APRM. As Commissioner Rebecca Kelly Slaughter stated in her accompanying remarks:

> Data abuses such as surreptitious biometric or *location tracking*, unaccountable and discriminatory algorithmic decision-making, or lax data security practices have been either caused by, exacerbated by, or are in service of nearly unfettered commercial data collection, retention, use, and sharing. [emphasis added] It is up to the Commission to use the tools Congress explicitly gave us, however rusty we are at wielding them, to prevent these unlawful practices.[44]

State Laws and Cases

As a result of the disjointed nature of federal oversight of privacy law, much of the general privacy law in the United States is being addressed at the state level. For example, every state has its own version of a data breach law, which requires organizations to take action, such as notifying the affected party or the state attorney general if certain designated personal information is accessed by an unauthorized third party.

Also, states have coordinated among themselves to bring actions against technology companies for privacy violations, including location privacy. For example, in 2022 Google paid $392 million to settle a claim brought by a coalition of states attorneys general that it collected and sold location data even after a consumer had turned off the location tracking feature.[45] In addition, Google reportedly agreed to make its location-tracking practices clearer.

There is also a growing trend at the state level to adopt comprehensive data protection laws. Many of these laws are modeled after the General Data Protection Regulation in Europe which came into effect in 2018. The first of these state laws was the California Consumer Privacy Act (CCPA), which came into effect in January 1, 2020. CCPA, and its subsequent amendments and regulations, grants citizens of California broad rights with respect to their data. Under CCPA, businesses are required to provide consumers with the right to opt out of the sale of their personal information, including precise geolocation data, and to provide notice about the collection and sharing of

44 Federal Trade Commission. (2022). *Statement of commissioner Rebecca Kelly Slaughter: Regarding the commercial surveillance and data security advance notice of proposed rule-making*. Retrieved January 1, 2024, from www.ftc.gov/system/files/ftc_gov/pdf/RKS%20ANPR%20Statement%2008112022.pdf.

45 NPR. (2022). *Google pays nearly $392 million to settle sweeping location-tracking case*. Retrieved January 1, 2024, from www.npr.org/2022/11/14/1136521305/google-settlement-location-tracking-data-privacy.

this information. Additionally, businesses must also implement reasonable security measures to protect consumers' personal information and to properly dispose of the information when it is no longer needed. Subsequently, other states, including Virginia, Colorado, Utah, and Connecticut, adopted similar laws.

The geospatial community faces several challenges with regard to the regulation of location information at the state level. First, the patchwork of laws requires that companies that do business in more than one state must do a state-by-state analysis as to whether location information is protected. If so, they then must compare the different definitions to see if and how they might apply. Another challenge is that a definition may have unintended consequence. For example, there is no indication that the Virginia law is intended to cover data collected from satellites. However, the definition is broad enough that it could be construed to do so by a judge or regulator.

In 2023, the State of Washington passed a law that further highlights the complexity of location privacy.[46] The My Health My Data Act (MHMD) was passed to give consumers more control over data that was related to health care, but not protected at the federal level by HIPAA. It applies to any person or entity that collects, uses, or discloses consumer health data. Consumer health data is defined as personal information that is linked or reasonably linkable to a consumer and that identifies the consumer's past, present, or future physical or mental health status and includes geolocation data. Geolocation data is defined as "precise location information that could reasonably indicate a consumer's attempt to acquire or receive health services or supplies."

MHMD gives consumers several rights with respect to their health data, including the right to

- access their health data
- correct any inaccuracies in their health data
- delete their health data
- restrict the collection, use, or disclosure of their health data
- opt out of the sale of their health data
- file a complaint with the state if they believe their health data has been mishandled

MHMD also requires companies that collect, use, or disclose consumer health data to take steps to protect the security of that data.

Massachusetts has also addressed the intersection of health data and location information. However, in this instance it was the state attorney general that took action by entering into a settlement agreement which restricted

46 Washington State Legislature. (n.d.). Chapter 19.373 RCW: Washington My Health My Data Act.

a company from using geofencing technology in the state.[47] Massachusetts' Attorney General brought the action when learning that the company was using geofencing technology to collect location data that was being sold to third parties. These third parties then sent texts and advertisements to the phones of women in family planning facilities, encouraging them to not have an abortion. Massachusetts alleged the use of this technology was an unfair or deceptive act or practice in violation of its consumer protection laws as it intruded upon a consumer's private health or medical affairs or status and/or results in the gathering or dissemination of private health or medical facts about the consumer without their consent. In the settlement agreement the company agreed not to use the geofencing technology either directly or indirectly through others, in the vicinity of any medical center located in Massachusetts to infer the health status, medical condition, or medical treatment of any person.

Data Broker Laws

Another set of state privacy laws that will likely impact some sectors of the geospatial ecosystem are what are commonly referred to as "data broker laws." Vermont's data broker law defines a data broker "as a business, or unit or units of a business, separately or together, that knowingly collects and sells or licenses to third parties the brokered personal information of a consumer with whom the business does not have a direct relationship."[48] It covers data that "alone or in combination with the other information sold or licensed, would allow a reasonable person to identify the consumer with reasonable certainty." While the Vermont law does not specifically state that location data is covered, the preamble to the law references concerns associated with location information.[49]

The law imposes several requirements upon data brokers, including

- registering with the Vermont Secretary of State annually
- maintaining certain minimum data security standards
- prohibitions on fraudulently acquiring certain types of data or using such data to commit bad acts

47 Office of the Attorney General. (2017). *AG reaches settlement with advertising company prohibiting 'geofencing' around Massachusetts healthcare facilities*. Retrieved January 1, 2024, from www.mass.gov/news/ag-reaches-settlement-with-advertising-company-prohibiting-geofencing-around-massachusetts-healthcare-facilities.

48 9 V.S.A. §§ 2430, 2433, 2446 and 2447.

49 Vermont General Assembly. (2018). *ACT 171 as enacted*. Retrieved January 1, 2024, from https://legislature.vermont.gov/Documents/2018/Docs/ACTS/ACT171/ACT171%20As%20Enacted.pdf.

California has a similar law which applies to certain businesses who sell personal information that they did not collect directly from the individuals.[50]

State Drone Laws

States are also moving more quickly than the federal government when addressing location privacy concerns associated with new technologies. For example, many states have passed laws to protect their citizens privacy from being violated by drones. Some of these laws address concerns regarding trespass.[51] Others prohibit the use of drones to conduct surveillance without a person's consent.[52] Some require law enforcement agencies to obtain a warrant before using drones for surveillance purposes.[53] Florida's law is perhaps the most expansive, as it provides that

> For purposes of this section, a person is presumed to have a reasonable expectation of privacy on his or her privately owned real property if he or she is not observable by persons located at ground level in a place where they have a legal right to be, regardless of whether he or she is observable from the air with the use of a drone.[54]

Conclusion

Location privacy is a dynamic area of geospatial law. Geospatial professionals should monitor developments in privacy law at both the federal and state levels. In addition, they should be mindful of legal developments across the broad spectrum of technologies that collect location information, as concepts of location privacy may develop through a variety of scenarios.

50 Cal. Civ. Code Section 1798.99.80 et. seq.
51 See e.g., Va. Code. § 18.2–121.3.
52 See e.g., W. Va. Code § 61–16–2.
53 See e.g., Va Code §19.2–60.1.
54 Fla Stat. §934.50.

4 Data Quality and Liability Considerations

Introduction

As discussed throughout the book, geospatial information (e.g., datasets, maps, images, etc.) is versatile. A map or a single dataset can be used in a wide range of applications. This versatility is one of the reasons geospatial information is such a powerful tool. But from a legal standpoint, this versatility means that there's greater risk when an organization uses or shares this information as data may appear usable for a particular application, but it may not have the necessary attributes. For example, it may not be accurate enough, precise enough, complete enough or timely enough for a particular use. If someone gets injured because of poor quality data, the issue then becomes which party is responsible?

In the past, the liability risks associated with geospatial information quality were more manageable. Due in part to the limited number of data types and the small size of the geospatial ecosystem, there was much greater certainty as to how data would be used and by whom. Most of the users were geospatial professionals themselves, so they presumably understood the limitations of data quality and the associated risks. In addition, most applications were in the business to business (B2B) or business to government (B2G) context. As will be discussed later, it is often easier to allocate liability risks in a B2B or B2G context than in a business to consumer (B2C) relationship.

However, as the types and amount of geospatial information grows, as the responsibility for geospatial information management gets pushed deeper into organizations, and as geospatial information is being used in more real-time decision-making, the liability risks associated with data quality become greater. As a result, the challenge for geospatial professionals will increasingly be how to mitigate the liability risks associated with data quality. This chapter will focus on data quality and the associated liability issues. The purpose of this chapter is three-fold. First, it is intended to help the reader understand the concepts of liability from a legal standpoint. The second is to help the reader understand the impact that these issues currently have and will have in the future on geospatial information management. Finally, the chapter will highlight some of the ways in which geospatial professionals can mitigate the potential liabilities associated with data quality.

DOI: 10.4324/9781003329961-4

Unique Characteristics of Geospatial Information

There are a number of unique characteristics of geospatial information that need to be considered in any discussion of data quality and liability. These include the following:

Wide Variety of Data Sources and Types – As noted previously, there are numerous types of geospatial information. There are also a wide range of sources for data, including surveyors, drone and satellite operators, satellite navigation (satnav) providers, and location-based service providers. Technologies are being developed that will make it easier and cheaper to collect and process more types of geospatial information, such as hyperspectral data. While organizations understand that these data types must be processed and integrated into operations differently, they often don't appreciate that they also raise different legal risks.

Role of Metadata – Metadata, essentially data about data, is an important component in most applications that use geospatial information. However, like with geospatial information in general, the types and qualities of metadata vary. Therefore, special attention often needs to be given to the role metadata in an application, as incomplete or inaccurate metadata can have a significant impact on data quality. However, rarely is metadata considered from a legal context.

Geospatial Information Services – In many instances, geospatial information is integrated into a service, such as in navigation, rather than simply delivered as a stand-alone product. As a result, the user may not even know the extent geospatial information is being used. Moreover, if a problem does occur, it may be difficult to determine whether the cause was due to poor data quality or to a software or hardware failure. It will be important to allocate these risks between all the parties involved.

Role of Standards – Standards often play an important role in the collection, use, and distribution of geospatial information. In any assessment of data quality, it will be important to understand whether applicable standards were followed and how they were addressed from a legal standpoint (e.g., in contract or law.).

Potential Sources of Liability Involving Data Quality

There are several liabilities that can arise pertaining to data quality. It is important for geospatial professionals to understand each and how they could arise in order to take the appropriate steps to mitigate. These include the following:

Contractual Liability: One significant risk that an organization can face is through its contracts or agreements with other parties. Failure to meet its contractual obligations, such as delivering accurate data or complying with the restrictions of use in a data sharing agreement, can result in contractual liability.

The key elements of contractual liability include the following:

- *Existence of a Contract*: There must be a valid contract between the parties that creates a legal obligation to perform certain services or actions.
- *Breach of Contract*: One of the parties must have failed to meet the terms of the contract.
- *Damages*: There must be actual harm or damage suffered as a result of the breach, such as increased costs, lost profits, or damage to reputation.
- *Causation*: The breach of contract must have been the cause of the other party's harm or damage.

These contractual obligations can arise in several contexts involving geospatial information. One is through affirmative statements in an agreement as to the quality of the information. As will be discussed in Chapter 7 these statements are generally known as representations and warranties and can take many forms. Express warranties are statements made by the seller (or licensor) that essentially guarantees certain characteristics or qualities of the product or service. For example, a contract may include a statement as to the resolution of electro-optical image to be delivered. Or it may state that a licensed dataset includes all of the geospatial information that is required for a particular application.

However, even if an organization does not make affirmative representations and warranties, in some instances the law may impose them. For example, most states have adopted the Uniform Commercial Code (UCC). Article 2 (Sale of Goods) of the UCC provides that for the sale of a product, certain warranties are assumed to be included unless they have been expressly waived. These warranties include merchantability[1] and fitness for a particular purpose[2]. The implied warranty of merchantability generally is stated as follows:

> Unless excluded or modified, a warranty that the goods shall be merchantable is implied in a contract for their sale if the Seller is a merchant with respect to goods of that kind.

In addition, the UCC provides that other implied warranties for merchantability may arise from "course of dealing between the parties or usage of trade within the industry" (UCC § 2–314). Similarly, the implied warranty of fitness for a particular purpose provides

> [w]here the Seller at the time of contracting has reason to know any particular purpose for which the goods are required, and that the buyer

1 Uniform Commercial Code (UCC) Section 2–314.
2 Uniform Commercial Code (UCC) Section 2–315.

> is relying on the Seller to select or furnish suitable goods, there is unless excluded or modified . . . an implied warranty that the goods shall be fit for such purposes.
>
> (UCC § 2–315)

One of the difficulties associated with respect to applying such implied terms to geospatial information products is that the use of geospatial information in most commercial contexts is relatively new. As a result, it is not clear how courts will apply these legal concepts in a dispute. For example, is there yet an "ordinary purpose" for which geospatial information is used? Similarly, what constitutes "fitness" of geospatial information for a particular purpose from a legal standpoint? Failure to meet these obligations can result in liability for breach of warranty or other claims. These can be both costly to a business and harmful to its reputation. As a result, it is important that geospatial organizations have clear contracts or agreements and documentation outlining which warranties apply, as well as to have quality control measures in place to ensure that the product or service meets the required standards.

Negligence

Another potential source of liability for geospatial information providers is the concept of negligence. There are essentially four elements to a claim of negligence. These are as follows:

1. Duty of care – the data provider must have a duty of care to the party claiming to be injured.
2. Breach – the data provider must have breached that duty.
3. Causation – the breach of the duty of care must have been the proximate cause of the injury; and
4. Damages – the party claiming injury must have suffered damage.

One of the challenges in a geospatial information context is determining whether a duty of care exists to the injured party. In the case *De Bardeleben Marine Corp v. U.S.*, in finding that the U.S. government had a duty of care to mariners, the court stated as follows:

> If a newspaper prints incorrect information, if a scientist publishes careless statements in a treatise or if an oil company prints an inaccurate road map, they cannot be 'liable' to those of the general public who read their works *absent some special relationship between the writer and reader.*[3] [emphasis added]

3 451 F2nd (5th Cir. 1971).

Therefore, with respect to geospatial information products or services, courts generally look to see if there is a 'special relationship' between the parties such that a duty of care is created. Factors that a court will consider include whether the information was specially communicated to the injured party and whether the data provider knew the specific purpose for which the injured party sought the information.

Negligence claims involving the duty of care and geospatial information quality arise in several different contexts. One such context is when there are errors in the data, or the data is not complete. For example, in *Southern Natural Gas Company v. Pontchartrain Materials Inc.*, the U.S. government was found liable for a portion of the damages that resulted from a dredge hitting an underground gas pipeline.[4] The dredging company had relied in part on a chart prepared by the U.S. government that had failed to adequately mark the pipelines on the chart. (It is important to note that charts did contain a warning that there may be certain uncharted submerged pipelines, but that the warning was not specific enough with regards to this type of pipeline.) However, in *Korean Air Lines Disaster of September 1, 1983*, the court found that a mapmaker did not have a duty of care to put a warning on an aeronautical chart that an aircraft may be shot down without advanced warning if it infringes upon another country's airspace, even if the chart included an airspace of a hostile country.[5]

Another element to a negligence claim is that the negligent act must be the proximate cause of the injury. In many instances it can be difficult to determine whether the error or defect was the proximate cause of the injury. For example, in *McCain v. Florida Power Corporation* the court found that the failure of Florida Power to accurately mark its underground power cables on a map was the proximate cause of injury McCain suffered when he struck the cables when using a trencher in reliance on the map.[6] Alternatively, in *AHV Properties v. Columbia Gas*, the court ruled that a utility was not negligent for only generally marking the location of its pipeline assets because industry practice was that it would not only accurately map those assets when specifically asked by a developer.[7] Since it had not been asked to do so by the plaintiff, it was not liable for the plaintiff's damages in relying on the map.

Product Liability

The Restatement of the Law (Second) Torts is a treatise that sets forth the principles of common law torts such as product liability. Section §402A provides that a person who sells any product in a defective condition unreasonably

4 711 F.2d 1251 (5th Cir. 1983).
5 597 F. Supp 619 (D.D.C., 1984).
6 593 So. 2d 500 (1992).
7 963 F. Supp. 460 (E.D. Pa, 1996).

dangerous to the user or consumer or to his property is subject to liability for physical harm thereby caused to the ultimate user or consumer, or to his property, if:

(a) the Seller is engaged in the business of selling such a product, and
(b) it is expected to and does reach the user or consumer without substantial change in the condition in which it is sold.[8]

The rule applies although (a) the Seller has exercised all possible care in the preparation and sale of his produce and (b) the user or consumer has not bought the product from or entered into any contractual relation with Seller. As a result, a plaintiff only needs to show (i) the defective condition, (ii) that it was unreasonably dangerous, and (iii) that it caused the physical harm. The duty of care is to any reasonably foreseeable member of the public that might be harmed. Since fault is not a required element of the cause of action, waivers and disclaimers generally are not relevant or invalid.

To date, geospatial information product liability claims primarily have dealt with defects in aeronautical charts. For example, in *Saloomey v. Jeppsen & Co.*, the court found that aeronautical maps are a product subject to strict product liability.[9] The court stated that by publishing and selling the charts, "Jeppesen undertook a special responsibility, as seller, to ensure that the consumers will not be injured by the use of the charts." The court added that "Jeppesen is entitled – and encouraged – to treat the burden of accidental injury as cost of production to be covered by liability insurance."

Similarly, in *Brocklesby v. U.S.*, the publisher of aeronautical charts was found liable for damages that resulted from an airline crash that resulted from errors in an aeronautical chart.[10] The court found that the charts were products and subject to a product liability claim even though the errors in the chart were based entirely on data provided by the government, not generated by the chart maker. In *Aetna Casualty and Surety Co. v. Jeppesen & Co.*, Jeppesen, a maker of aeronautical charts, was found liable for damages when a graphical image of a runway approach was misrepresented on an aeronautical chart even though the accompanying data on the chart was correct.[11]

Professional Liability – Geospatial professionals can also be held liable for errors or omissions in the data they collect or the analysis they perform. For example, if a surveyor uses geospatial technology to create a property boundary map and makes an error, they could be held liable for any resulting property disputes or legal claims. In *Rozny v. Mansul*, a surveyor guaranteed

8 Restatement (Second) of Torts § 402A cmt. b (Am. Law Inst. 1965).
9 707 F.2d 671 (2d Cir. 1983).
10 767 F.2d 1288 (9th Cir. 1985).
11 642 F.2d 339.

on the face of a plat its accuracy.[12] A homeowner, relying upon the plat's accuracy, extended a portion of his house and garage onto his neighbor's adjacent land. The Court held that the surveyor, not the homeowner, was required to reimburse the neighbor for the encroachment.

Steps to Mitigate or Allocate Liability Risks

As described previously, there are several potential liability risks associated with developing products and services that use geospatial information. These risks are likely to increase, particularly as geospatial information is being used in real-time decision-making by autonomous or semiautonomous products. However, there is risk inherent in any business. Therefore, it is important to balance the benefits of geospatial technology and the many applications which use geospatial information against the possible risks. Geospatial professionals can take steps to make these risks more manageable as well as to limit damages (both to third parties and to their organization). These steps include the following:

Education – One of the greatest risks associated with data quality is that many of those involved in the process are unaware of geospatial technology and the unique qualities associated with geospatial information. Therefore, it is important to educate professionals and consumers alike on the technology and its uses, to include judges, regulators, and policymakers so that a clear and consistent legal and policy framework can develop. Without such education, it will be difficult to properly implement many of the measures described in the next section.

Legislation – Laws can protect geospatial organizations from certain liabilities associated with geospatial information. For example, the National Geospatial-Intelligence Agency (NGA) is protected from certain civil claims related to geospatial information. Specifically, 10 U.S.C. § 456 provides that "[n]o civil action may be brought against the United States on the basis of the content of geospatial information prepared or disseminated by the National Geospatial-Intelligence Agency." In Arizona

> [a] public agency that shares geospatial information of which it is the custodian is not liable for errors, inaccuracies or omissions and shall be held harmless from and against all damage, loss or liability arising from any use of geospatial information that is shared.[13]

12 250 N.E.2d, 656, (III. 1969).
13 A.R.S. § 37–178.

Similarly, in Kansas, a government entity or an employee acting within the scope of the employee's employment is not liable for damages resulting from

> providing, distributing or selling information from geographic information systems which includes an entire formula, pattern, compilation, program, device, method, technique, process, digital database or system which electronically records, stores, reproduces and manipulates by computer geographic and factual information which has been developed internally or provided from other sources and compiled for use by a private agency, either alone or in cooperation with other public or private entities.[14]

Legislation also can be passed to protect businesses from liability associated with data quality. For example, after the cases described in the previous section in which chart makers were found liable for errors in aeronautical charts, Congress gave the Federal Aviation Administration (FAA) the ability to indemnify chart makers against claims made for certain defects. Specifically, 49 U.S.C. § 44721 provides that

> [t]he Government shall make an agreement to indemnify any person that publishes a map or chart for use in aeronautics from any part of a claim arising out of the depiction by the person on the map or chart of a defective or deficient flight procedure or airway if the flight procedure or airway was –
>
> (1) prescribed by the Administrator [of the Federal Aviation Agency],
> (2) depicted accurately on the map and chart; and
> (3) not obviously defective or deficient.

Use of Standards and Policies – Standards or guidelines are also a useful method to improve and maintain geospatial information quality. Both data providers and data customers can use such standards and guidelines to increase the chance that proper geospatial information quality is attained. Compliance with standards and guidelines can also be a method to allocate the risks. However, it is important to note that such standards and guidelines will often have limited value if applied too broadly because the level and type of quality will vary depending upon the application and the customer. As a result, standards and guidelines have been developed for specific applications that use geospatial information. For example, the

14 K.S.A. 75-6104.

International Hydrographic Organization has developed standards for hydrographic surveying.[15]

Contracts – Another way in which parties can avoid or limit liability is through contract. There are several contract provisions that can be used. These include the following:

Disclaimers – A party can include express language in their agreements that specifically disclaims representations or warranties with respect to the data, including "fitness for a particular purpose" or "merchantability." Alternatively, a geospatial organization might include a disclaimer stating that the data or information provided is for informational purposes only and not intended to be used as the sole basis for any decision-making. It is important to note that such waivers and disclaimers may not always be enforceable against consumers. For example, in some jurisdictions, if a product is considered inherently dangerous, a consumer's waiver of representation or warranties or release of claims is not valid.

Limitation of liability clauses – Another common method to limit a geospatial organization's liability is to cap the amount of damages that a party can recover in case of a breach of contract or other liabilities. The limitation of liability clauses can also exclude liability for certain types of damages, such as indirect or consequential damages.

Indemnification clauses – Indemnification clauses provide that one party will hold harmless and compensate another party for certain types of losses, damages, or claims. For example, a geospatial organization might require its customers to indemnify it from any third-party claims for damages arising out of a client's use of geospatial information or services.

Limiting the scope of work – A useful way to limit liability is to carefully define the scope of services or work in a contract. For instance, a geospatial organization might only agree to provide specific services or data or certain services or data may be specifically excluded from the scope of the contract.

Insurance requirements – A geospatial organization can require its clients to obtain insurance coverage that specifically covers the risks associated with the geospatial products or services. This can help to mitigate the organization's liability exposure by transferring some of the risk to the client's insurer.

Risk Assessments – Experience from other industries suggests there are certain steps a company that collects or uses geospatial information can take

15 International Hydrographic Organization. (2008). IHO standards for hydrographic surveys. *International Hydrographic Organization*. Retrieved January 21, 2024 from https://iho.int/uploads/user/pubs/standards/s-44/S-44_5E.pdf.

to ensure proper quality of its products and services. One of the first and most important steps is to conduct a risk assessment. The purpose of the risk assessment is to identify potential hazards and risks associated with the intended use (or reasonably anticipated misuse) of a product or service. A risk assessment can be helpful in both implementing steps to reduce injury (and therefore potential liability claims) and in building a defense in the event a claim is made and litigation arises.

Data Audits – Data audits are another means for a geospatial organization to ensure that geospatial information being used is of sufficient quality for the purposes for which it is being marketed. A data audit involves a review of vendors, internal policies and procedures, and customers. For example, a data audit can be used to ensure that third party vendors have complied with contractual obligations with respect to data quality and in accordance with relevant laws and regulations. A data audit also can be used to develop and evaluate adequate internal processes and controls in anticipation of any third-party investigations. It might also review marketing and advertising materials to make sure that the organization can comply with all statements.

Insurance – Another means in which an organization can and should protect itself against liability is through insurance. There are several types of insurance to consider, including general liability insurance, professional liability insurance, and cyber insurance.

Quality and Control Programs – Quality control and quality assurance are critical components of the geospatial ecosystem and play an essential role in reducing the risk of liability for geospatial professionals and organizations. By implementing rigorous quality control and quality assurance procedures, geospatial professionals can minimize the likelihood of errors or inaccuracies in their work and, therefore, reduce the risk of liability.

Professional Certification/Licensing – Certification and licensing of geospatial professionals can reduce the risk of liability by ensuring that those who are providing geospatial services have the necessary knowledge, skills, and training to perform their work competently and ethically.

Conclusion

Liability issues associated with data quality will increase as geospatial information becomes an integral component in critical and time-sensitive decisions. As a result, geospatial professionals will need to understand the risks to protect themselves and their respective stakeholders (organizations, managers, employees, shareholders, etc.) from liability. This will require understanding potential sources of liability associated with the applicable geospatial information and how it will be used. It also requires an understanding of what steps can be taken to limit risk.

5 The U.S. Government as a Regulator

Introduction

The U.S. government plays several roles in the geospatial ecosystem. One of the most critical is as regulator of both geospatial technologies and geospatial information. This chapter highlights the various ways the U.S. government regulates the geospatial community and the impact it has on geospatial information management. Not surprisingly, much of this regulation occurs at the federal level. However, this chapter will explain that states can also play an important role.

It is crucial to note that this chapter does not address the U.S. government's role as a regulator concerning data protection/privacy, as that is discussed in significant detail in Chapter 3. Additionally, while several laws and policies mentioned in this chapter have national security implications, the majority of the national security concerns associated with geospatial information management are detailed in Chapter 6.

The geospatial ecosystem comprises numerous technologies and spans various industry sectors. Due to the structure of the U.S. government, this results in many federal agencies having the authority to regulate activities related to the collection, use, storage, or distribution of geospatial information. The responsible regulatory agency will vary depending upon several factors, including (i) the type and nature of technology (e.g., satellite or mobile device), (ii) the intended user of the technology or geospatial information (e.g., business or consumer), and (iii) the United States' international obligations (e.g., treaties). In some instances, multiple agencies may have a role in the same geospatial activity. Moreover, regulations may occur at different points in the geospatial information life cycle (e.g., collection, analysis, storage, distribution). Consequently, it is often necessary for stakeholders to identify all possible regulators to determine which apply. Failing to do so could result in the inability to obtain a necessary license, fines, or other disciplinary actions.

Additionally, this chapter will explore how rapid advancements in geospatial technology and applications that use geospatial information are increasing the number of government agencies with regulatory responsibility. For

DOI: 10.4324/9781003329961-5

instance, regulations issued by the Department of Energy on smart grids could include requirements to protect certain information tied to a location for privacy reasons. Similarly, the Department of Transportation likely will play a regulatory role with respect to the quality of geospatial information used in autonomous vehicles. While businesses within these respective industries will understand the need to comply with such laws and regulations, more traditional geospatial companies also may need to be aware as they could become subject to these laws. For example, a geospatial vendor in the autonomous vehicle supply chain could be subject to data quality or privacy requirements.

This chapter will explain how regulators often try to balance the benefits of a certain technology with the perceived risks. These risks will vary depending upon the technology and/or the application. They will also vary depending upon the regulator and its mission. However, it is also important to keep in mind that incumbent professionals or businesses that feel threatened by new geospatial technology or competitors will raise concerns with regulators over matters such as safety.

Earth Observation Satellites

Space law is an entire legal discipline and encompasses multiple aspects, many of which are unrelated to geospatial law. For example, issues in space law include activities on the moon, human space flight, and mining of asteroids. Nonetheless, since space activities play an essential role in geospatial information management, impacting both Earth observation and positioning, navigation, and timing (PNT), space law overlaps with geospatial law.

The Remote Sensing Principles

As with most legal issues associated with space, the legal and regulatory framework is a mixture of treaties, international law, and norms along with national legal and policy frameworks. The starting point for Earth observation is the Principles Relating to Remote Sensing of the Earth from Outer Space (the "Remote Sensing Principles").[1] The Remote Sensing Principles were adopted by the United Nations in 1986, when a limited number of countries had Earth observation satellites. As a result, one of the primary purposes of the Remote Sensing Principles was to assuage developing states concerned that developed states would use the technology to exploit their resources.

1 G.A. Res. 41/65, U.N. GAOR, 41st Sess., Supp No. 53, at 115 U.N. Doc. A/RES/41/65 (1986).

The principles establish that

- remote sensing activities should be carried out for the benefit of all countries and in accordance with international law and based on the principles that all nations and people have sovereignty over their own wealth and natural resources
- nations carrying out remote sensing activities should promote international cooperation and maximize the availability of benefits of remote sensing activities
- a sensed nation should have access to remote sensing information collected from its territory
- states should bear international responsibility for the remote sensing activities of both government and non-government actors within their jurisdiction

Because the Remote Sensing Principles are not a treaty, they are nonbinding on countries. However, the U.S. government has incorporated some of the provisions into the licensing process for commercial satellite remote sensing activities. For example, under U.S. law, U.S. licensees must:

> [u]pon request, offer to the government of any country (including the United States) unenhanced data collected by the system concerning the territory under the jurisdiction of such government without delay and on reasonable terms and conditions, unless doing so would be prohibited by law or license conditions.[2]

Commercial Satellite Remote Sensing in the United States

In order to understand the current state of U.S. law regarding commercial satellite remote sensing, it is important to understand how the history and the concerns are associated with the technology. The U.S. government started using Earth observation satellites for defense and intelligence purposes during the Cold War. However, it was not until 1978 that President Carter issued presidential directives that declassified the fact that the U.S. government was using remote sensing satellites recognized that both civil and commercial remote sensing sectors could play a role in Earth observation, subject to government "authorization, supervision, and regulation," and permitted "federal earth imaging from space" at resolutions at or better than ten meters "when appropriate and when such needs are justified and assessed in relation to civil benefits and national security and foreign policy concerns."[3]

2 15 CFR 960.8(c).

3 Presidential Directive/NSC-37 National Space Policy. *Jimmy Carter Library and Museum*. Retrieved January 12, 2024, from www.jimmycarterlibrary.gov/sites/default/files/pdf_documents/assets/documents/directives/pd37.pdf.

This tension between the policy of successive administrations to support the development of a commercial remote sensing industry and the associated national security concerns associated with the evolving technology continues today.

1984 Land Remote Sensing Commercialization Act

As discussed in Chapter 10, the Landsat program has been a mainstay of U.S. Earth observation efforts since 1972. However, in the late 1970s and early 1980s, there was a growing sense within the U.S. government that the program was not being fully utilized. Successive administrations had explored commercializing the Landsat program, and in 1984 Congress passed the Land Remote Sensing Commercialization Act of 1984 (the "1984 Act").[4] The 1984 Act provided for a phased commercialization of the Landsat program. In addition, the 1984 Act included provisions that permitted the licensing of commercial satellite remote sensing systems.

The Land Remote Sensing Policy Act of 1992

The commercialization of Landsat was soon recognized as a failure. The Land Remote Sensing Policy Act of 1992 (the "1992 Act") replaced the 1984 Act and returned Landsat to public control.[5] It also authorized the Department of Commerce to issue regulations pertaining to licensing of commercial satellite remote sensing systems. In 1993, President Clinton issued the first commercial satellite imaging license to WorldView.

In 1994, the Clinton Administration issued Presidential Decision Directive-23 (PDD-23).[6] Its stated goal was to "support and enhance U.S. industrial competitiveness in the field of remote sensing space capabilities while at the same time protect U.S. national and foreign policy interests."

PDD-23 set forth a number of obligations upon commercial satellite remote sensing operators, including maintaining a record of satellite operations and not changing the orbital characteristics of a satellite without prior approval from the Secretary of Commerce. It also introduced the concept of "shutter control," in which operators could be directed by the Secretary of Commerce to limit the collection and/or distribution of imagery due to national security concerns or international obligations. This process was formalized by a Memorandum of Understanding among the Departments of State, Defense, Commerce, Interior, and the Intelligence Community.

Due to particular concerns regarding Israel, the Kyl-Bingaman Amendment, introduced as part of the National Defense Authorization Act for 1997,

4 Pub. L. 98–365. (1984).

5 Public Law 102–555. (Oct. 28, 1992). Land Remote Sensing Policy Act of 1992.

6 Presidential Decision Directive-23 (PDD-23). *Clinton presidential libraries*. Retrieved January 12, 2024, from https://clinton.presidentiallibraries.us/items/show/12747.

prohibited the U.S. government from granting a commercial remote license for collecting or disseminating satellite imagery of Israel at a higher resolution than is available from commercial sources outside the United States.[7]

The U.S. Commercial Remote Sensing Policy issued by the Bush Administration, superseded PDD-23.[8] In support of its stated goal of advancing and protecting "U.S. national security and foreign policy interests by maintaining the nation's leadership in remote sensing space activities, and by sustaining and enhancing the U.S. remote sensing industry," it directed the federal government to "rely to the maximum practical extent on U.S. commercial remote sensing space capabilities for filling imagery and geospatial needs for military, intelligence, foreign policy, homeland security, and civil users."

Specifically, the policy directed the U.S. government to

- focus government remote sensing space systems on meeting needs that cannot be effectively, affordably, and reliably satisfied by commercial providers
- develop a long-term, sustainable relationship between the federal government and the U.S. commercial remote sensing space industry
- provide a timely and responsive regulatory environment for licensing the operations and exports of commercial remote sensing space systems
- enable U.S. companies to compete successfully as a provider of remote sensing space capabilities for foreign governments and foreign commercial users, while protecting national security and foreign policy

SPD-2 Streamlining Regulations on Commercial Use of Space (2018)

The legal and policy framework for U.S. commercial satellite remote sensing remained essentially unchanged until the Trump Administration issued U.S. Space Policy Directive 2 (SPD-2).[9] SPD-2 directed federal agencies to review and improve the existing regulatory framework for space activities. One of the reasons for this change was the sense that the U.S. lead in space was decreasing, including in the sector of satellite Earth observations.

With respect to commercial satellite remote sensing, SPD-2 provided that

> Within 90 days, the Secretary of Commerce shall review the regulations adopted by the Department of Commerce under Title II of the Land

7 National Defense Authorization Act for Fiscal Year 1997, Pub. L. No. 104–201, § 1064 (1996).

8 Commercial Remote Sensing Policy Retrieved January 12, 2024, from the National Environmental Satellite, Data, and Information Service website at www.nesdis.noaa.gov/s3/2021-08/Commercial%20Remote%20Sensing%20Policy%202003.pdf.

9 Space Policy Directive-2, Streamlining Regulations on Commercial Use of Space. Retrieved January 12, 2024, from https://trumpwhitehouse.archives.gov/presidential-actions/space-policy-directive-2-streamlining-regulations-commercial-use-space/.

> Remote Sensing Policy Act of 1992 (51 U.S.C. § 60101 et seq.) for consistency with the policy and shall rescind or revise those regulations, or publish for notice and comment proposed rules rescinding or revising those regulations, as appropriate and consistent with applicable law.

After a preliminary draft of proposed regulations was criticized by industry as being too restrictive, the Department of Commerce updated its regulations for issuing a commercial remote sensing license in May 2020 (the "New Regulations").[10] The New Regulations were meant to improve the licensing process and to make U.S. commercial satellite remote sensing companies more globally competitive. One of the most significant changes was the introduction of a three-tier licensing scheme.

- Tier 1 systems are those whose capabilities to collect unenhanced data are substantially the same as those of systems not licensed by NOAA.
- Tier 2 systems are those which U.S. commercial providers subject to NOAA's jurisdiction have similar capabilities to collect unenhanced data, but not foreign commercial operators.
- Tier 3 systems are those offering capabilities to collect unenhanced data that are not available from either foreign or U.S. commercial providers.

In keeping with the intent of SPD-2, the National Oceanic and Atmospheric Administration's (NOAA) authority to regulate companies operating Tier 1 and Tier 2 systems is limited. Licensees of Tier 2 systems can be required to (i) obtain the consent of the owner of any satellite orbiting Earth before imaging it and (ii) notify the Secretary of Commerce five days before conducting such an imaging operation. In addition, a licensee of a Tier 2 system must comply with NOAA directives to limit operations due to national security concerns.

However, NOAA has much broader authority to regulate companies operating Tier 3 systems. In addition to Tier 2 restrictions, NOAA can impose temporary license conditions on Tier 3 systems. These restrictions can include restricting or limiting the frequency of collection over a certain area or limiting the spectral bands used for collection.

Guidance Circulars

The New Regulations were generally seen by industry as a significant improvement. However, as with most laws and regulations, several questions arose. As a result, beginning in 2022 NOAA's Commercial Remote Sensing Regulatory Affairs (CRSRA) issued a series of guidance circulars intended to address frequently asked questions by applicants and licensees. While such

10 15 CFR Part 960.

guidance circulars do not have the force and effect of law, they provide clarity on NOAA's position on several important issues.

Key guidance issued by NOAA includes the following:

- *Clarifying the Definition of U.S. Person and "Operating" a System*[11]

The 1992 Act applies to persons that are "subject to the jurisdiction and control of the United States." Therefore, a license is required for (i) any entity or individual, of any nationality, operating the system inside the U.S., or (ii) a U.S. person operating the system anywhere in the world. One of the challenges frequently faced by companies operating remote sensing systems based outside the U.S. is determining at what point their operations in the U.S. subject them to NOAA licensing requirements. For example, this guidance circular addressed a hypothetical in which a German corporation with a U.S. subsidiary collects imaging orders from U.S.-based customers. This guidance circular states that if the orders are sent to the foreign parent company, which tasks the system with collecting the data required to fulfill the order and could decline to fulfill the order for any reason, the foreign parent company would be considered the "operator." As a result, neither the U.S. subsidiary nor the German parent would require a NOAA license. Similarly, this guidance circular states that a license is not required if a foreign company, as part of its ground station network, uses a ground station in the U.S. to send commands and receive data from a remote sensing system, as the authority to send commands controlling the remote sensing instrument is made from a location outside the United States.

- *Determining Radar Quality*[12]

The New Regulations require categorization of licenses based on the availability (or lack thereof) of comparable data to that which the system being licensed will produce. A question that was frequently asked when determining whether a prospective licensee should receive a Tier 2 or Tier 3 license was defining "substantially the same" with respect to radar because of its unique characteristics. In this guidance, NOAA has stated that it will use a single metric – the Radar General Image Quality Equation, or RGIQE – to

11 National Environmental Satellite, Data, and Information Service. (2022, April 1). GC No: 960.2-1 Instruments used primarily for mission assurance or other technical purposes. *National Environmental Satellite, Data, and Information Service.* Retrieved January 12, 2024, from www.nesdis.noaa.gov/s3/2022-04/Guidance_%20Mission%20Assurance%20%20040122.pdf.

12 National Environmental Satellite, Data, and Information Service. (2022, March 31). GC No: 960.6-1 Calculation and use of the RGIQE metric for SAR Tiering. *National Environmental Satellite, Data, and Information Service.* Retrieved January 12, 2024, from www.nesdis.noaa.gov/s3/2022-04/SAR%20RGIQE%20Metric%20guidance%20032321_0.pdf.

compare SAR systems, rather than a weighting scheme to account for spatial resolution and signal strength. NOAA stated in this guidance that it believes RGIQE bridges the gap between hardware and data, that is, between instrument capability (the way NOAA's regulations require it to evaluate U.S. licensees) and data quality (the way NOAA's regulations require it to evaluate foreign data availability).

- *Mission Assurance*[13]

The New Regulations exclude NOAA's regulatory jurisdiction over sensors or other instruments on a spacecraft that are used primarily for mission assurance or other technical purposes rather than remote sensing. A system that only contains mission assurance instruments does not require a license from the Department of Commerce. This guidance circular states that the mission assurance exception is focused on the actual use of the instrument (e.g., mission assurance), rather than the instrument's objective description. It states that in determining whether the "mission assurance" exemption applies, NOAA focuses on whether the instrument is "primarily" used for the listed purpose. If there are multiple uses of an instrument, factors to be considered in determining whether a license is required include

- how much time the operator spends using the instrument for each purpose
- what the operator would use the instrument for if it could only use it for one purpose
- the typical reason in the space industry for using such an instrument

PNT

The National Defense Authorization Act for Fiscal Year 1998, as published under Title 10 United States Code § 2281, gives the Secretary of Defense the authority to operate and sustain GPS for both military and civil purposes, free of charge to users. However, as with many geospatial technologies, both civil and defense agencies have significant roles in GPS operations.

For example, the Secretary of Defense is directed to coordinate with the secretary of transportation on GPS requirements and augmentation and with the secretary of commerce and others to facilitate civil and commercial uses. The Council on Oversight of the Department of Defense Positioning, Navigation, and Timing Enterprise is responsible for overseeing the Department

13 National Environmental Satellite, Data, and Information Service. (2022, April 1). GC No. 960.2–1 instruments used primarily for mission assurance or other technical purposes. *National Environmental Satellite, Data, and Information Service*. Retrieved January 12, 2024, from www.nesdis.noaa.gov/s3/2022-04/Guidance_%20Mission%20Assurance%20%20040122.pdf.

of Defense PNT enterprise, including services provided to civil, commercial, scientific, and international users.[14]

In 2004, the U.S. Space-Based Positioning, Navigation, and Timing Policy (the "2004 Policy") was published. It replaced the Presidential Decision Directive/National Science and Technology Council-6, U.S. Global Positioning System Policy, dated March 28, 1996. The 2004 Policy established guidance and implementation actions for space-based PNT programs, augmentations, and activities for U.S. national and homeland security, civil, scientific, and commercial purposes.

President Trump issued Space Policy Directive 7 (SPD-7) to replace the 2004 Policy.[15] Its stated goal was to maintain United States leadership in the service provision and responsible use of global navigation satellite systems, including GPS and foreign systems. SPD-7 addressed a wide range of matters associated with civil and commercial use of PNT, including

- providing continuous worldwide access to U.S. space-based GPS services and government-provided augmentations, free of direct user fees
- operating and maintaining GPS in accordance with U.S. law to satisfy civil, homeland security, and national security needs
- improving capabilities to deny hostile use of U.S. government space-based PNT services, without unduly disrupting civil and commercial access to civil PNT services
- enhancing the performance of U.S. space-based PNT services

Crewed Aircraft

Crewed aircraft are currently used to collect numerous types of geospatial information. In the U.S., aircraft operations are subject to the laws of the Federal Aviation Administration (FAA), which are covered by CFR Title 14 Chapter 1. Similar to space law, aviation law is a distinct and complex body of law separate from geospatial law. However, there are important areas of overlap.

Two of the most important of these areas for a geospatial professional are airworthiness certificates and airspace. An airworthiness certificate is an FAA document that grants authorization to operate an aircraft in flight. There are two types: Standard Airworthiness Certificate and Special Airworthiness Certificate. Each has separate requirements. A Special Airworthiness Certificate is required for aerial surveying.[16]

14 10 U.S.C. § 2279b.

15 Space Policy Directive 7. (2021, January 15). Retrieved January 12, 2024, from https://trumpwhitehouse.archives.gov/presidential-actions/memorandum-space-policy-directive-7/.

16 14 CFR. Part 91 General Operating & Flight Rules.

Airspace in the U.S. is heavily regulated. There are two categories of airspace: regulatory and nonregulatory. Within each category there are four types. These types are based on the complexity or density of aircraft movements, the nature of operations, the level of safety required, and national and public interest. Most operations involving the collection of geospatial information will occur in regulatory airspace. The regulatory requirements will vary depending upon the airspace class.[17]

Drones

In 2012, Congress passed the FAA Modernization and Reform Act of 2012, directing the FAA to develop a comprehensive plan to safely accelerate the integration of unmanned aircraft systems (UAS), or drones, into the National Airspace System (NAS). In 2016, pursuant to that authority, the FAA issued Part 107 to Title 14 of the Code of Federal Regulations. Part 107 establishes rules for the operation of small drones that do not require FAA airworthiness certification.

Part 107 restricted a number of drone operations unless a waiver was obtained from the FAA. These include operations (i) over persons, (ii) at night, (iii) generally above an altitude of 400 feet above ground level, or (iv) beyond visual line-of-sight. The FAA has made it somewhat easier to operate small drones without obtaining a waiver, but progress remains slow.

Surveying

States play an important role in regulating surveying activities. Each state has legislation pertaining to application procedures, examinations, and the conferring of licenses to practice professional surveying.

The subject of surveyor licensing is outside the scope of this book as many of the aspects are related to real property law. However, as a growing number of geospatial technologies are enabling non-professional surveyors to collect accurate geospatial information with little or even no training, there is a growing tension between surveying and geospatial professionals. This is why, as in many areas of laws, the definition of what constitutes the practice of surveying within a state is so critical. For example, in Virginia the "practice of land surveying" includes

> surveying of areas for a determination or correction, a description, the establishment or reestablishment of internal and external land boundaries, or the determination of topography, contours or location of physical improvements, and also includes the planning of land and subdivisions thereof. The term "planning of land and subdivisions thereof"

17 See e.g., 14 CFR Part 71.

> shall include, but not be limited to, the preparation of incidental plans and profiles for roads, streets and sidewalks, grading, drainage on the surface, culverts and erosion control measures, with reference to existing state or local standards.[18]

In the state of Washington, surveying is defined as

> assuming responsible charge of the surveying of land for the establishment of corners, lines, boundaries, and monuments, the laying out and subdivision of land, the defining and locating of corners, lines, boundaries, and monuments of land after they have been established, the survey of land areas for the purpose of determining the topography thereof, the making of topographical delineations and the preparing of maps and accurate records thereof, when the proper performance of such services requires technical knowledge and skill.[19]

North Carolina has a much more prescriptive definition. It defines the practice of land surveying as

> a. Providing professional services such as consultation, investigation, testimony, evaluation, planning, mapping, assembling, and interpreting reliable scientific measurements and information relative to the location, size, shape, or physical features of the earth, improvements on the earth, the space above the earth, or any part of the earth, whether the gathering of information for the providing of these services is accomplished by conventional ground measurements, by aerial photography, by global positioning via satellites, or by a combination of any of these methods, and the utilization and development of these facts and interpretations into an orderly survey map, plan, report, description, or project. The practice of land surveying includes the following:
>
> 1. Locating, relocating, establishing, laying out, or retracing any property line, easement, or boundary of any tract of land;
> 2. Locating, relocating, establishing, or laying out the alignment or elevation of any of the fixed works embraced within the practice of professional engineering;
> 3. Making any survey for the subdivision of any tract of land, including the topography, alignment and grades of streets and incidental drainage within the subdivision, and the preparation and perpetuation of maps, record plats, field note records, and property descriptions that represent these surveys;

18 Va. Code Ann. § 54.1–400 (2023).
19 RCW 18.43.020 (2023).

4. Determining, by the use of the principles of land surveying, the position for any survey monument or reference point, or setting, resetting, or replacing any survey monument or reference point;
5. Determining the configuration or contour of the earth's surface or the position of fixed objects on the earth's surface by measuring lines and angles and applying the principles of mathematics or photogrammetry;
6. Providing geodetic surveying which includes surveying for determination of the size and shape of the earth both horizontally and vertically and the precise positioning of points on the earth utilizing angular and linear measurements through spatially oriented spherical geometry; and
7. Creating, preparing, or modifying electronic or computerized data, including land information systems and geographic information systems relative to the performance of the practice of land surveying.[20]

Of note for geospatial professionals, the surveying profession is challenging the use of technologies such as drones for surveying-like activities without a state-issued survey license.[21]

Conclusion

The federal government regulates a number of technologies and activities that play an important role in geospatial information management. The agencies responsible for these regulations vary, depending upon the technology and the perceived risks. Geospatial professionals must understand the regulatory environment in which they operate and how the legal and policy framework impacts their organizations' mission. In some professions, such as surveying, understanding state regulatory requirements is also essential.

20 N.C. Gen. Stat. § 89C-3 (2023).
21 See e.g., *360 Virtual Drone Services LLC v. Ritter* (5:21-cv-00137) District Court, E.D. North Carolina.

6 Security Laws and Policies Associated With Geospatial Technology

Introduction

There are a wide range of national and homeland security issues associated with geospatial information. One of the primary reasons for these issues is that many geospatial technologies have military and intelligence roots. As a result, agencies within these parts of government approach geospatial information with a great deal of ambivalence. On the one hand, certain offices within these agencies see tremendous value in acquiring as much geospatial information as possible. However, other offices within the same agencies have concerns about the technology or geospatial information ending up in the hands of adversaries or other bad actors.

Understandably, the U.S. government gives these agencies great deference when they express national security and homeland security concerns. This chapter will discuss the restrictions that are imposed on geospatial technology and information due to potential homeland and national security concerns. It will also explain the impact these restrictions have on the geospatial ecosystem.

Export Controls

One area of national security law with particular significance for the geospatial community is export controls. There are several significant export regimes that must be considered. However, before beginning, it is important to understand the definition of export under U.S. law. An export is broadly defined under U.S. law. It includes (1) an actual shipment or transmission out of the United States; (2) releasing or otherwise transferring technical data to a foreign person in the United States (a "deemed export"); (3) transferring registration, control, or ownership of any aircraft, vessel, or satellite by a U.S. person to a foreign person; (4) releasing or otherwise transferring a defense article to an embassy in the United States; or (5) performing a defense service on behalf of, or for the benefit of, a foreign person, whether in the United States or abroad.[1] As a result, geospatial technology

1 22 C.F.R. § 120.

DOI: 10.4324/9781003329961-6

or associated technical data does not have to leave the U.S. to be considered an export under U.S. law.

If technology or technical data which would otherwise be subject to U.S. export control laws is imported into the U.S. it also becomes subject to U.S. export control laws. This "re-exporting" of technology or technical data is subject to the same restrictions, including transfers to a foreign person in the United States.

Export controls in the U.S. are covered by a wide range of laws and regulations. Two of the most important are the International Traffic in Arms Regulations[2] and the Export Administration Regulations (EAR).[3] An understanding of each is essential for any geospatial professional working on matters with potential defense or intelligence applications.

ITAR

ITAR controls items, information, or activities that a foreign military could use to harm U.S. interests. It covers both products – for example, defense articles – and defense services. The Directorate of Defense Trade Controls (DDTC) in the Department of State is responsible for ITAR, pursuant to the authority granted under the Arms Export Controls Act.[4] Because of the nature of the items covered by ITAR, it is considered a very restrictive export regime.

The United States Munitions List (USML) is a list of articles, services, and related technical data that are subject to ITAR. All items and services described on the USML require export authorization by the Department of State and either a license – for products – or an approved agreement – such as a Technical Assistance Agreement (TAA) – for services.

The USML is divided into 21 categories of defense articles and services, several of which pertain to geospatial technology.[5] For example, Category XV of the USML pertains to "Spacecraft systems and related articles." This category includes items that are used in the development, production, and operation of spacecraft and satellites, including satellites for both civilian and military use. These categories also include technical data, software, and services that are directly related to items listed on the USML and are necessary for the design, development, production, operation, installation, maintenance, repair, overhaul, or refurbishing of defense articles.

Similarly, Category XI covers "Military Electronics," which includes sophisticated sensors (i.e., certain radar and "[e]lectronic systems, equipment or software, not elsewhere enumerated in this subchapter, specially designed

2 22 U.S.C. § 2778.
3 15 CFR Subtitle B Chapter VII Subchapter C.
4 Foreign Military Sales Act, Pub. L. No. 90–629, 82 Stat. 1320 (1968).
5 Title 22 Chapter I Subchapter M Part 121.

for intelligence purposes that collect, survey, monitor, or exploit, or analyze and produce information from, the electromagnetic spectrum regardless of transmission medium"). Of note, even if the technology, such as a sensor, is not subject to ITAR, the export of certain data and information products generated from the sensor might still qualify as a defense service.

EAR

The EAR controls items and technologies that are considered to be "dual use." Dual use items and technologies are those that can be used for commercial and/or military use. These items are detailed in the Commerce Control List – a list of commercial or dual use items (i.e., commodities, software, and technology) subject to the EAR licensing regime of the Bureau of Industry and Security (BIS), which is part of the Department of Commerce.[6] The CCL is divided into ten broad categories. Each CCL category is subdivided into five product groups. An item that falls into a specific category and product group is given an Export Control Classification Number. An ECCN categorizes items based on the nature of the product, that is, type of commodity, software, or technology, and its respective technical parameters. Items subject to the EAR but not identified on the CCL are identified by the designator "EAR99." EAR99 items generally consist of low-technology consumer goods and do not require a license in many situations.

Export Control Reform Act of 2018

Under Section 1758 of the Export Control Reform Act of 2018, Congress directed the Department of Commerce to adopt new export controls on "emerging and foundational technologies."[7] On January 6, 2020, BIS adopted export licensing requirements on certain artificial intelligence software used to automate the analysis of geospatial imaging.[8] The software subject to the new export licensing requirements was limited to geospatial imagery "software" "specially designed" for training a Deep Convolutional Neural Network to automate the analysis of geospatial imagery and point clouds, and having all of the following:

1. Provides a graphical user interface that enables the user to identify objects (e.g., vehicles, houses, etc.) from within geospatial imagery and point clouds in order to extract positive and negative samples of an object of interest;

6 Title 15 Subtitle B Chapter VII Subchapter C Part 774.
7 50 U.S.C. Ch 58.
8 Addition of Software Specially Designed To Automate the Analysis of Geospatial Imagery to the Export Control Classification Number 0Y521 Series. *Federal Register, 85*(459).

2. Reduces pixel variation by performing scale, color, and rotational normalization on the positive samples;
3. Trains a Deep Convolutional Neural Network to detect the object of interest from the positive and negative samples; and
4. Identifies objects in geospatial imagery using the trained Deep Convolutional Neural Network by matching the rotational pattern from the positive samples with the rotational pattern of objects in the geospatial imagery.

A license was required for most exports and reexports of this geospatial software. Of note this licensing requirement expired in January 2023 and was not extended by BIS.

Denied Persons List

The Denied Persons List (DPL) is a list of individuals and entities that are prohibited from receiving U.S. exports due to their involvement in activities such as terrorism, weapons proliferation, money laundering, and human rights abuses.[9] The DPL is maintained by BIS. Businesses are required to check the DPL before engaging in any transactions with parties on the list, to ensure compliance with U.S. laws and regulations. For example, U.S.-licensed commercial remote sensing companies must have a mechanism in place to make sure that image products and services are not exported to companies and individuals on this list. Violations can result in severe penalties, including fines and even imprisonment.

The U.S. also imposes trade sanctions on individuals, entities, and countries as a means of exerting pressure or influence on a target country or group. For example, the Specially Designated Nationals List, which is maintained by the U.S. Department of Treasury's Office of Foreign Assets Control, includes individuals and entities that are subject to sanctions under various U.S. laws and regulations.[10] Violating sanctions regulations can also result in significant penalties.

Concerns Over Specific Geospatial Technologies

There are a number of other national security laws and regulations that have a significant impact on the collection and use of geospatial information.

9 See e.g., Bureau of Industry and Security. (2024). *Denied persons list*. Retrieved January 12, 2024, from www.bis.doc.gov/index.php/policy-guidance/lists-of-parties-of-concern/denied-persons-list.

10 See e.g., Office of Foreign Assets Control. (2024). *Specially Designated Nationals and blocked persons list (SDN)*. Retrieved January 12, 2024, from https://ofac.treasury.gov/specially-designated-nationals-and-blocked-persons-list-sdn-human-readable-lists.

Commercial Satellite Imagery

As noted in Chapter 5, the U.S. government has had security concerns with the commercial satellite imagery industry. When the commercial satellite imagery was first being developed, the defense and intelligence communities were worried that images of U.S. troops, facilities, and weapon systems would be available to adversaries. As a result, the Commercial Remote Sensing Policy Act of 1992 (the "Act") requires a commercial remote sensing provider to obtain a license from the National Oceanic and Atmospheric Administration (NOAA).[11] The Act, and the associated regulations,[12] impose a number of restrictions on commercial providers that were intended to address national security concerns. For example, the application is subject to review by a number of federal agencies. These agencies subsequently entered into a memorandum of understanding (MOU) to address how to handle a dispute as to whether a commercial remote sensing license should be granted or what restrictions to impose on operations.

NOAA also has limited authority to impose restrictions limiting the resolution of the imagery that can be collected and "shutter control" – that is, the ability to prohibit collection over specific areas at specific times. In addition, Congress passed the Kyl-Bingaman Amendment, which restricts U.S. companies collecting imagery of Israel that is better than can be collected by non-U.S. commercial systems.[13]

Over the years, the commercial remote sensing industry expressed a number of concerns about the license process. The concerns included the length of the time required for a license to be granted and the lack of transparency in the process. Industry complained that these put U.S. companies at competitive disadvantage with foreign companies. As a result, in 2020, NOAA issued new regulations meant to improve the licensing process and to make U.S. companies more competitive.

One of the most significant changes was the creation of three tiers of commercial remote sensing systems:

- Tier 1 systems are those whose capabilities to collect unenhanced data are substantially the same as those of systems not licensed by NOAA.
- Tier 2 systems are those which U.S. commercial providers subject to NOAA's jurisdiction have similar capabilities to collect unenhanced data, but not foreign commercial operators.
- Tier 3 systems are those offering capabilities to collect unenhanced data that are not available from either foreign or U.S. commercial providers.

11 Public Law 102–555, 106 Stat. 4163 (1992).
12 15 CFR 960.
13 Public Law 104–201, Section 1064 (1996).

NOAA's authority to regulate licensees of Tier 1 and Tier 2 systems is limited. Licensees of Tier 2 systems can be required to (i) obtain the consent of the owner of any satellite orbiting Earth before imaging it, and (ii) notify the Secretary of Commerce five days before conducting such an imaging operation. In addition, a Tier 2 licensee must comply with NOAA directives to limit operations due to national security concerns.

However, NOAA has much broader authority to regulate licensees of Tier 3 systems. In addition to Tier 2 restrictions, NOAA can impose temporary license conditions on Tier 3 systems. These restrictions can include restricting or limiting the frequency of collection over a certain area or limiting the spectral bands used for collection.

Global Positioning System (GPS)

Historically, there have also been significant security concerns associated with GPS. In 1990 the Department of Defense introduced Selective Availability – a feature that intentionally degraded the precision of the GPS signals for non-military users to prevent adversaries from using GPS for military or other malicious purposes. In 2000, President Clinton ended Selective Availability on the grounds that the commercial benefit of GPS was greater than the potential risks that were associated with the technology. This resulted in an explosion of commercial applications using GPS data, such as navigation, transportation, and emergency services.

However, the U.S. continues to limit the construction of satellite positioning ground monitoring stations within the country. The president may not authorize or permit the construction of a global navigation satellite system ground monitoring station directly or indirectly controlled by a foreign government in the United States unless the Secretary of Defense and the director of National Intelligence jointly certify to the appropriate congressional committees that such ground monitoring station will not possess the capability or potential to be used for the purpose of gathering intelligence in the United States or improving any foreign weapon system.[14]

Drones

Drones are another example of a technology with numerous benefits for the geospatial community that also raises a number of security and safety concerns. As discussed in further detail in Chapter 5, some of these concerns relate how to integrate drones into the national airspace without jeopardizing the safety of crewed aircraft. However, the Department of Defense, the FBI, and the Department of Homeland Security have national security

14 10 U.S.C. §2279d.

concerns, based in part on how terrorists and insurgents are using the technology across the globe.

Due to these concerns, the Federal Aviation Administration (FAA) has been slow in adopting regulations that facilitate the integration of drones into the national airspace. In an effort to address some of these concerns, the FAA published a Notice of Proposed Rulemaking (NPRM) on Remote Identification of Unmanned Aircraft Systems on December 31, 2019. The final rule was published in the Federal Register on January 15, 2021.[15] It requires drone pilots to meet certain remote identification requirements to broadcast identification and location information about the drone and its control station.

Another national security associated with drones pertains to relations with China. Specifically, the Department of Defense has been concerned that Chinese-made drones operated in the U.S. were sending sensitive information back to China. For example, in 2017, the Department of Defense banned the use of drones manufactured by the Chinese company DJI.[16] The DoD cited "cybersecurity risks" as the reason for the ban and said that the DJI drones "are the most widely used non-program of record commercial off-the-shelf UAS," but also that "the data collected, stored, and potentially transmitted by these UAS is potentially vulnerable to unauthorized access and exploitation." The DJI drones were banned from use by any DoD component or any DoD contractor. The DoD also encouraged other government agencies to review their use of DJI drones and consider similar bans.[17] Subsequently, in 2022, the Department of Defense included DJI on a list of companies from which it is prohibited contracting with or procuring goods, services, or technology from pursuant to Section 1260H of the National Defense Authorization Act for Fiscal Year 2021.[18]

Open Data

As discussed in several chapters throughout this book, the U.S. government has had a policy of making government data open and available to the public.

15 14 CFR Parts 1, 11, 47, 48, 89, 91, and 107.

16 Holdeman, E. (2024, January 8). Federal government will require purchase of made in America drones. *Government Technology*. Retrieved January 12, 2024, from www.govtech.com/em/emergency-blogs/disaster-zone/federal-government-will-require-purchase-of-made-in-america-drones.

17 Kesteloo, H. (2018, June 7). Department of Defense bans the purchase of commercial-over-the-shelf UAS, including DJI drones effective immediately. *DroneDJ*. Retrieved January 12, 2024, from https://dronedj.com/2018/06/07/department-of-defense-bans-the-purchase-of-commercial-over-the-shelf-uas-including-dji-drones/.

18 U.S. Department of Defense. (2022, October 5). *DOD releases list of People's Republic of China (PRC) military companies in accordance with section 1260H of the National Defense Authorization Act for Fiscal Year 2021*. Retrieved January 12, 2024, from www.defense.gov/News/Releases/Release/Article/3180636/dod-releases-list-of-peoples-republic-of-china-prc-military-companies-in-accord/.

However, after the terrorist attacks on September 11, 2001, the U.S. government reviewed the extent publicly available geospatial information was a national security risk. Several studies were conducted. One such study was commissioned by the Federal Geographic Information Committee (FGDC) which published a detailed report on the issues, including a decision tree for agencies to consider in determining whether to restrict the availability of geospatial information.[19]

In 2002, the Homeland Infrastructure Foundation-Level Data (HIFLD) Subcommittee was established to improve the collection, processing, sharing, and protection of homeland infrastructure geospatial information across multiple levels of government and to develop a common foundation of homeland infrastructure data. The members of the subcommittee include the DoD, DHS, NGA , and USGS.

The objectives of the subcommittee include identifying any geospatial information that should not be made publicly available due to security concerns. As a result, there are currently two subsets of data. The HIFLD Open data portal contains national foundation-level geospatial critical infrastructure data within the public domain that can be useful to support community preparedness, response and recovery, etc. HIFLD Secure consists of For Official Use Only and other restricted data layers. Government credentials are required to access HIFLD Secure.

Security concerns associated with open data also arise at the state level. For example, in *County of Santa Clara v. California First Amendment Coalition*, one of the issues was whether a county GIS base map was exempt from California's public records laws due to national security concerns.[20] Specifically, Santa Clara County argued that the records were "protected critical infrastructure information," exempt under the Critical Infrastructure Information Act of 2002. The court rejected this claim, finding that since the County had summitted the information to the federal government rather than received it, the act did not apply.[21]

Classified Contracts

As noted previously, the Department of Defense and the Intelligence Community are significant customers for businesses that sell geospatial products and services. Not surprisingly, the contracts to purchase these products and services often involve access to classified information. A business wishing to

19 *Guidelines for Providing Appropriate Access to Geospatial Data in Response to Security Concerns (June 2005) ASPRS*. Retrieved January 12, 2024, from www.fgdc.gov/policyandplanning/Access%20Guidelines.pdf.

20 170 Cal.App.4th 1301 (2009).

21 Slip opinion Retrieved January 19, 2024, from https://web.archive.org/web/20110727145237/www.opendataconsortium.org/ODC%20website%20additions/CFAC-Santa%20Clara%20County%20%20Appeals%20Court%20decision.pdf.

have access to classified information must receive a Facility Clearance (FCL). The process and requirements for obtaining an FCL are set forth in the National Industrial Security Program Operating Manual (NISPOM), codified at 32 Code of Federal Regulations (CFR) Part 117. An FCL and approved safeguarding of classified information is required for firms bidding on a contract in which they will be provided with classified information. A company must be sponsored for an FCL either by the U.S. Government or by another cleared company that wants to utilize the company as a subcontractor on a classified contract. A company works with the Defense Counterintelligence and Security Agency (DCSA) to comply with applicable requirements.

Cybersecurity

The U.S. government is increasingly concerned about cybersecurity threats. This includes threats from foreign countries, as well as those from terrorists and criminals. As a result, as will be discussed in more detail in Chapter 8, businesses that sell geospatial products and services to the U.S. government are increasingly required to comply with a series of cybersecurity requirements. For example, both the Federal Acquisition Regulation (FAR) and the Defense Federal Acquisition Regulation Supplement (DFARS) include provisions related to cybersecurity that contractors and suppliers must comply with when doing business with the federal government.

FAR 52.204–21 (Basic Safeguarding of Covered Contractor Information Systems) requires that all contractors and suppliers handling federal information not intended for public release to implement basic security measures to protect the information from unauthorized access, use, or disclosure. Measures required to be taken by government contractors include

- limiting information system access to authorized users or devices
- limiting information system access to the types of transactions and functions that authorized users are permitted to execute
- authenticating (or verifying) the identities of users or devices, as a prerequisite to allowing access to organizational information systems
- limiting physical access to organizational information systems, equipment, and the respective operating environments to authorized individuals
- monitoring, controlling, and protecting organizational communications
- updating malicious code protection mechanisms when new releases are available
- performing periodic scans of the information system and real-time scans of files from external sources as files are downloaded, opened, or executed

DFARS Clause 252.204–7012 (Safeguarding Covered Defense Information and Cyber Incident Reporting) is a much more comprehensive list of obligations and requirements for contractors and suppliers. It also references NIST SP 800–171 "Protecting Controlled Unclassified Information in Nonfederal

Systems and Organizations." NIST SP 800–171 is a set of security guidelines and best practices developed by the National Institute of Standards and Technology (NIST). The guidelines are intended to help organizations protect Controlled Unclassified Information (CUI) that is stored, processed, or transmitted on nonfederal information systems and networks. CUI is a term used to describe information that is not classified but still requires protection from unauthorized disclosure. CUI includes a wide range of information that is sensitive but not classified, such as personal information, critical infrastructure, trade secrets, and other types of sensitive information. Many types of geospatial information are considered as CUI.

The program to protect CUI was established by Executive Order 13556 – Controlled Unclassified Information, which created a framework for the identification, safeguarding, dissemination, and declassification of CUI.[22] The program is governed by the National Archives and Records Administration (NARA) and is intended to provide a consistent and standardized way of handling unclassified information that requires protection.

The Cybersecurity Maturity Model Certification (CMMC) is a certification framework being created by the DoD to ensure that contractors and suppliers that handle CUI for the DoD comply with appropriate cybersecurity practices. The CMMC framework is designed to provide a tiered system of certification levels, ranging from basic cyber security measures to more advanced information security practices. When implemented, CMMC will impose a number of requirements for contractors, including in some cases third-party audits.

In addition, NOAA has issued a guidance circular related to cybersecurity for commercial remote sensing satellites. It provides guidance to the commercial remote sensing industry on how to protect their systems from cybersecurity threats.[23] The guidance circular recommends that organizations implement a risk management program that includes regular risk assessments, incident response planning, and security testing. It also recommends that organizations implement security controls such as access controls, encryption, and firewalls to protect their systems from cyber threats. Additionally, the guidance circular also provides recommendations on how to comply with relevant laws and regulations such as the Federal Information Security Modernization Act (FISMA) and the Cybersecurity Information Sharing Act (CISA).

22 https://obamawhitehouse.archives.gov/the-press-office/2010/11/04/executive-order-13556-controlled-unclassified-information. Accessed January 12, 2024.

23 NOAA GC. (2022). *960.9(a)-1 "Guidance for licensees–Cybersecurity measures"*. Retrieved January 12, 2024, from www.nesdis.noaa.gov/s3/2022-10/960.9%20(a)%201-3%20and%20960.10%20(a)(1)(i)%20(A%20&%20B)%20Guidance_%20Cybersecurity%20Measures_10032022.pdf.

Conclusion

Geospatial technology and information raise a number of national and homeland security concerns. In order to address these concerns, the U.S. has a number of laws and regulations that restrict the collection and distribution geospatial information. Several government agencies have roles in implementing these laws, which can be a challenge for geospatial companies, particularly for those wishing to do business with the government or internationally.

7 Licensing of Geospatial Information[1]

Introduction

License agreements play a critical role in the development of geospatial products and services. This chapter will explain how these legal agreements help protect the rights of both the creators and users of geospatial information. It will discuss some of the challenges in licensing of geospatial information due to the unique attributes of both the information and the geospatial ecosystem. The chapter will also provide an overview of the various types of geospatial licenses and key terms and conditions. It will then discuss licensing with the U.S. Government, open data licenses, and the consequences for not complying with licensing terms.

License Agreements for Geospatial Information

A licensing arrangement is more complicated from a legal standpoint than a sale transaction. In a sale, the buyer transfers ownership in the product. After the sale, the buyer is free to do what he or she wants with product. In a licensing arrangement, the licensor retains ownership in the item being licensed, but transfers to the licensee certain rights in the item, usually for a certain period of time and/or a certain use. As a result, the licensor has a vested interest in the licensee's use of the item. The license agreement is what describes each party's relative rights and obligation. Anything that is not included in the agreement is subject to the interpretation of a judge, jury, or regulator in the event of a dispute.

Licensing is very common in many parts of the technology sector, including in the geospatial ecosystem. For example, software is licensed by commercial entities to other commercial entities, government agencies as well as nongovernmental organizations (NGOs). However, as will be discussed later, licensing geospatial information raises some complex issues that do

1 For purposes of this chapter, the term "License Agreement" is used to describe any agreement which involves data sharing.

DOI: 10.4324/9781003329961-7

not arise in the software context and therefore are considered an area of geospatial law.

Geospatial information can be licensed in a variety of ways. The most common method is pursuant to a simple data license agreement, in which the licensing of the geospatial information is the primary purpose of the agreement. However, geospatial information also is increasingly being offered as part of other products and services, such as Software as a Service (SaaS), with the data sharing terms found in Terms of Service, the Terms of Use, or similar legal documentation. An organization will also need to grant certain rights in geospatial information when entering Data as a Service (DaaS) agreements or in a cloud hosting agreement.

As noted throughout this book, geospatial products and services increasingly are being created by aggregating different types of geospatial information. As in most instances, no one organization has all of the data it needs, businesses, government agencies, and NGOs alike need to obtain data from other parties. This generally is done through one or more license agreements.

Many of the legal issues addressed in this book should be considered when entering into a geospatial information license agreement as a licensee or a licensor. For example, does the licensor have sufficient intellectual property rights in the information to grant the license? Does the licensor have any legal responsibility if there are errors in the geospatial information? Alternatively, does a licensee have any responsibility to the licensor if a third party is injured by a service offered by the licensee that includes licensor's geospatial information? A well-crafted license agreement will address these issues and many more.

Role of a License Agreement

A license agreement serves many roles. From a legal standpoint, a license agreement sets forth the rights the licensor is granting the licensee. This facilitates the sharing of information between parties so that each can better achieve their objectives. It also allocates legal and business risks between the parties.

Both the licensor and the licensee must understand their respective rights in geospatial information so as to be able to comply with all legal and contractual obligations. For example, if a licensee wishes to store geospatial information in the cloud, it is important to ensure that such storage is permitted under the license agreement, as some licensors require their information to be stored locally. It is also important for the licensee to ensure that such storage is permitted under local law, as most license agreements include a provision for compliance with local law, and in some jurisdictions certain types of data cannot be stored outside the country.

Key Elements of a License Agreement

Regardless of its form, a license agreement should contain several key items. These include:

1. *A Detailed Description of the Geospatial Information Being Licensed* – It is important to accurately describe what geospatial information is being licensed. For example, if the licensed product is imagery, is the imagery raw or processed? If it is data, what type of data? Also, given the importance of metadata in the geospatial ecosystem, what, if any, metadata is being licensed?

In some instances, it can be useful to state what intellectual property rights the licensor has in the geospatial information being licensed. For example, if the licensor claims copyright over the information, it is useful to clearly state that in the license.

A clear, complete, and accurate description of the geospatial information is important as several provisions are tied to the geospatial information being licensed. Also, it puts the licensee on notice, as different types of geospatial information are subject to different legal and regulatory regimes. For example, some governments impose restrictions on imagery collected from unmanned aircraft systems (commonly known as drones) that do not apply to imagery collected from a manned aircraft or a satellite. As a result, a complete and accurate description can also help reduce future disputes between the parties.

2. *The Specific Rights That Are Being Granted to the Licensee* – A license also needs to state the specific rights that the licensor is granting the licensee and whether there are any limitations or associated requirements. For example, is the licensee receiving exclusive rights, or can the licensee grant the same or similar rights to another party?

The specific rights granted will depend upon various factors. These can include

- the type of geospatial information being licensed
- the licensor's intellectual property rights in the geospatial information
- how the geospatial information is going to be used by the licensee
- what other uses the licensor has or may have for geospatial information

In some cases, a license agreement might simply grant the licensee the right to "use" geospatial information. This is a broad term that has little legal meaning. As a result, the licensor may consider granting the licensee some or all of the bundle of rights typically associated with copyright protection, such as (i) the right to make a copy, (ii) the right to distribute or display the geospatial information, or (iii) the right to make a derivative work. In each case, it is important for the parties to have a clear understanding of the rights being granted and ensure those rights are accurately reflected in the license agreement.

As the definitions of some of these terms can vary, it is helpful to define them in the agreement to avoid any disagreement between the parties in the future. For example, defining what constitutes a permitted derivative product can be useful as there is very little law on this topic pertaining to geospatial information services and products.

The license agreement also should describe any requirements or restrictions associated with the rights granted. An example of a requirement would be requiring proper attribution if the licensee publishes the geospatial information. Such attribution might include that the information was owned (and if applicable, copyrighted) by the licensor.

There are many restrictions that a licensor may wish to impose in a license agreement. For example, it may limit the rights granted to a particular country or within a particular industry. The licensor may limit the form the licensee can produce products or services using the geospatial information (e.g., only in hard copy, so that the information is not easily copied by a third party).

The licensor may also wish to explicitly prohibit the licensee from using the geospatial information for certain applications for which the licensor does not believe the geospatial information is suited, or for which the risks (legal or business) are too great. For example, a license agreement may prohibit the licensee from using geospatial information for turn-by-turn navigation.

Other common restrictions include that the geospatial information

- can only be used internally
- may not be used for commercial purposes
- may not be used to compete with the licensor

3. *Appropriate Representations and Warranties* – As discussed in Chapter 3, a licensor might also be asked to make specific representations or warranties directly relating to the geospatial information. For example, a licensor may be asked to represent that it owns the geospatial information (or that it has the right under an agreement with the owner to license the geospatial information to the licensee for the purposes set forth in the license agreement).

   The warranty on the other hand generally is more forward-looking. It is essentially a promise by the licensor to address problems that may arise in the future, generally for a defined period of time. For example, a licensor might promise to replace the medium in which geospatial information was delivered 60 days after delivery. Also as noted in Chapter 4, warranties can be either expressed or implied. Express warranties are written into the license agreement and, in many instances, will relate directly to the geospatial information being licensed. There are several types of express warranties that a licensee might request from a licensor. These include the (i) accuracy, (ii) precision, (iii) completeness, (iv) timeliness, and/or (v) format of the geospatial information being licensed. Implied warranties are included in a commercial transaction, even if these warranties are not specifically set forth in the geospatial information license. If a licensor does not wish for these implied warranties to apply, it must clearly and specifically waive those in the license agreement.

4. *Requirements for Parties to Comply With Applicable Law* – A license agreement should include a section whereby both of the parties agree to abide by applicable laws, regulations, decrees, etc. This would require, for instance, the licensee only using the geospatial information in ways that comply with the laws of the jurisdiction(s) in which the geospatial information is being used. Such a section serves several purposes. One purpose is to remind the licensee that there may be laws it needs to consider before it is using geospatial information. In addition to putting the parties on notice to understand what laws might apply, it also is a way to allocate the risk in the event a law or regulation is violated. A "compliance with laws" section will become increasingly important in a geospatial information license agreement as more laws and regulations develop around the collection, use, storage and distribution of geospatial information. These include laws regarding privacy/data protection and national security. By implication, the license agreement also should state which jurisdiction's laws apply to the agreement itself.

Entering Into License Agreements With the U.S. Government

As will be discussed in greater detail in Chapter 9, selling products and services to the U.S. government is different than commercial sales. One of the biggest differences is that government procurements are subject to the Federal Acquisition Regulation (FAR). In addition, government agencies can have their own additional regulations. For example, the Department of Defense has the Defense Federal Acquisition Regulation Supplement (DFARS).[2]

The FAR and DFARS have several provisions that relate to licensing. For example, geospatial information is often considered "technical data" for government contracting purposes. Technical data is defined as "any recorded information of a scientific or technical nature (e.g., product

2 For purposes of this chapter the term FAR will be used to include FAR Supplements.

design or maintenance data, computer databases, and computer software documentation)."[3]

The rights the U.S. government receives in technical data depend upon the source of funding for the creation of the data. If the creation of the data was exclusively government funded, the government receives "unlimited rights."[4] An "unlimited rights" license means that the federal government can use, modify, reproduce, release, or disclose technical data or computer software in whole or in part, in any manner, and for any purpose whatsoever, and to have or authorize others to do so.

If the data was created using both government and private funds, then the government expects to receive "government purpose rights."[5] Government purpose rights "means the rights to use, modify, reproduce, release or disclose the technical data or computer software within the Government without restriction and outside the Government for a Government purpose." "Government purpose is any activity in which the federal government is a party, including cooperative agreements with international or multinational defense organizations or sales or transfers by the United States Government to foreign governments or international organizations." A government purpose license remains in effect for five years unless the parties negotiate a different period. Upon expiration of the five-year (or other negotiated) term, the federal government has "unlimited rights" in noncommercial technical data or noncommercial computer software.

If the data was created with no government funds (i.e., privately funded) but is not considered a commercial item, the government receives limited rights. "Limited rights means the rights to use, modify, reproduce, release, perform, display, or disclose technical data, in whole or in part, within the Government."[6]

However, it is important to note that the rights described previously apply to noncommercial items. Geospatial information that is a commercial item and can be licensed to the U.S. government under commercial licensing terms. Licensing of commercial geospatial information to the U.S. government is covered in more detail in Chapter 9.

Open Data Licenses

The Open Data Handbook defines open data as "data that can be freely used, re-used and redistributed by anyone – subject only, at most, to the

3 "Defense Federal Acquisition Regulation Supplement. (2023). Rights in Technical Data–Other Than Commercial Products and Commercial Services (252.227–7013)).
4 Code of Federal Regulations. § 227.7103–5(a), Title 48).
5 Code of Federal Regulations. § 227.7103–5(b), Title 48).
6 Code of Federal Regulations. § 227.7103–5(c) Title 48).

requirement to attribute and sharealike."[7] However, even though it is intended to be freely used, open data is licensed. For example, while users have "free, full and open access" to the European Union's Copernicus Sentinel satellite geospatial information, such use is subject to the terms of the "Legal Notice on the use of Copernicus Sentinel Data and Service Information found on the Copernicus webpage."[8] Similarly, Canada's Open Maps are published under the Open Government License – Canada.[9]

Likely the most common open data licenses for geospatial information are the Creative Commons suite of licenses[10] and Open Data Commons Open Database License (ODbL) v.1.0.[11] The Australian government publishes public data under a Creative Commons license, while the popular mapping community OpenStreetMap publishes its data under the ODbL.

A detailed analysis of the various license types is beyond the scope of this book, but it is worthwhile noting that open data licenses can have significant differences from a legal standpoint. For example, a "share-alike" provision requires the licensee to grant its users the same rights that it has received from the licensor. Therefore, when an organization chooses to make its data open, it still must consider what type of license it wishes to use.

Consequences of Violating Licensing Agreements

A licensee can suffer several negative consequences if it fails to comply with the terms of a license agreement. The most obvious penalty is that the licensor could cut off access to the geospatial information. The licensor might also sue the licensee for damages incurred by the breach. For example, if the licensee used the geospatial information in prohibited markets or for prohibited applications, the licensor might claim damages for lost business opportunity. If the licensee uses the geospatial information in ways that violate the licensor's copyright, the licensor might sue for damages from copyright infringement. Finally, if a licensee habitually violates license agreements, the licensee might suffer reputational damage. This would make it difficult to find organizations willing to grant it a license in the future.

7 Open Data Handbook. (n.d.). *What is open data?* Retrieved January 12, 2024, from https://opendatahandbook.org/guide/en/what-is-open-data/.

8 European Space Agency. (n.d.). *Sentinel data legal notice*. Retrieved January 12, 2024, from https://sentinel.esa.int/documents/247904/690755/sentinel_data_legal_notice.

9 Government of Canada. (n.d.). *Open Government Licence–Canada*. Retrieved January 12, 2024, from https://open.canada.ca/en/open-government-licence-canada.

10 Creative Commons. (n.d.). *Share your work*. Retrieved January 12, 2024, from https://creativecommons.org/share-your-work/cclicenses/#:~:text=Creative%20Commons%20licenses%20give%20everyone,creative%20work%20under%20copyright%20law.

11 Open Data Commons. (n.d.). *Open Database License (ODbL) 1.0*. Retrieved January 12, 2024, from https://opendatacommons.org/licenses/odbl/1-0/.

Conclusion

Many geospatial products and services involve aggregating geospatial information licensed from other parties. A geospatial information license agreement is a legal document in which the licensor grants rights in geospatial information to the licensee. The license grant can take several forms, but most include several key components. Geospatial license agreements will become increasingly important as new technologies use geospatial information in new and innovative ways.

8 Ethics and Other Nongovernmental Instruments

Background

While it is critical that geospatial professionals understand the legal framework within which they operate, it is also important for them to understand the role that nongovernmental instruments such as ethics play in geospatial information management. These instruments, which also includes standards and best practices, can play an important role. This chapter will begin by discussing several types of nongovernmental instruments. It will then include a deeper discussion on ethics and explore some of the ethical issues faced by geospatial professionals. It will then explain some of shortfalls in using ethics to address the legal issues that impact geospatial information management, including the relationship between law and ethics.

Nongovernmental Instruments

Instruments such as standards, norms, best practices, and ethics generally are nonbinding from a legal standpoint. However, they can provide many benefits in geospatial information management. One of the primary benefits is that they are much easier to develop and implement than laws and regulations. As a result, they can be more flexible, which makes them easier to adopt (i.e., because they are nonbinding, organizations are less concerned about the consequences for failing to abide). This also makes them much easier to modify than a law to adapt to new technologies or legal issues that may arise. They also can remain in force longer than a binding legal document such as a contract or license agreement. In addition, they can apply to both public and private sector organizations.

However, there also are several limitations that must be considered. Since these nonbinding instruments do not have the force of law, they generally cannot be enforced in a court. Also, they usually only apply to a limited group that has self-selected to abide by them; although market pressure and integrating nonbinding elements in formal legal instruments – such as including standards in contracts – can increase their adoption.

DOI: 10.4324/9781003329961-8

Standards

Standards are an example of nongovernmental instruments that play a significant role throughout the geospatial ecosystem. For example, the Open Geospatial Consortium has published standards that facilitate the sharing of geospatial information between organizations in different domains (e.g., maritime, aviation, etc.) and for various technologies (e.g., cloud, 3D)[1]. These standards have been adopted by thousands of organizations across the globe and are essential for the interoperability of geospatial technology and information. While non-legally binding on their own, they can become binding if a party agrees in a contract to use a particular standard.

Best Practices

Best practices also play an important role in geospatial information management. For example, the American Society for Photogrammetry and Remote Sensing (ASPRS) published both the "Guidelines for Procurement of Professional Aerial Imagery, Photogrammetry, Lidar and Related Remote Sensing Sensor-based Geospatial Mapping Services" (the "Professional Services Guidelines")[2] and the "Guidelines for Procurement of Commercial Products" (the "Commercial Products Guidelines").[3] The two guidelines were primarily intended to provide government agencies resources to help determine the best approach and methodology for procuring professional services and commercial products.

Ethics

The geospatial community has spent a considerable amount of time considering the role of ethics in geospatial information management. In fact, several professional organizations have developed their own set of ethics concerning geospatial matters. These include

- the ASPRS Code of Ethics[4]
- the Geospatial Information and Technology Association (GITA) Code of Ethics[5]

1 *Open Geospatial Consortium*. Retrieved January 21, 2024, from www.ogc.org/.

2 ASPRS. (2009). Guidelines for procurement of professional aerial imagery, photogrammetry, lidar and related remote sensing sensor-based geospatial mapping services. *ASPRS*. Retrieved January 12, 2024 from www.asprs.org/a/society/committees/standards/Procurement_Guidelines_w_accompanying_material.pdf.

3 APRS. (2014). ASPRS guidelines for procurement of geospatial mapping products and services. *ASPRS*. Retrieved January 21, 2024, from www.asprs.org/a/society/committees/standards/Combined_Procurement_Guidelines.pdf.

4 ASPRS. (2014). Code of ethics. *ASPRS*. Retrieved January 12, 2024, from www.asprs.org/a/publications/pers/2014journals/PERS_December_2014/HTML/files/assets/common/downloads/page0056.pdf.

5 GITA Code of Ethics. *GITA*. Retrieved January 21, 2024, from www.gisci.org/Ethics/Code-of-Ethics.

In addition, the Locus Charter has a stated goal of providing a common set of international principles to "help users of geospatial data make more informed decisions and provide the basis for communication with people affected by those decisions."[6] In addition, the role of ethics in the geospatial community is frequently discussed at geospatial conferences and taught in geospatial courses.

Ethics are an important consideration in the geospatial ecosystem. However, because they are nonbinding, they often have a limited impact. In addition, since geospatial technology and information is used in so many industries and professions around the globe, and for so many different applications, developing a comprehensive code of ethics that can be used across the entire geospatial community is difficult, if not impossible.

Ethics can be defined as principles of human values, morals, and approved behavior.[7] As a tool to guide a person or organization in deciding whether an action (or inaction) is right or wrong, ethics can play an important role in all aspects of society. Ethics can also promote civic responsibility among citizens and institutions.[8]

One of the primary reasons that the geospatial community has focused on ethics is that the law has failed to keep up with advancements in geospatial technology. This is not surprising in the abstract as the law often tends to be reactive rather than proactive. However, it is particularly the case for geospatial technology, due in part to the dual use of geospatial technology and geospatial information. This duality can be summarized as follows:

> At every stage of our interactions with geospatially-informed materials and events, there are decisions being made that have the potential to bring or cause harm to individuals, organizations, institutions, and society. Individual privacy is a hot topic, kept in the limelight partly because of the way our phones (cars, computers, etc.) record and publicize our daily whereabouts. Other digital technologies are part of the overall privacy picture too: the many tens of thousands of drones that are being put into flight each month and the new satellites tasked with capturing increasingly high-resolution global activity.[9]

The COVID-19 pandemic also raised ethical considerations regarding the role of geospatial information. Geospatial information played an important

6 EthicalGeo. (2019). *EthicalGeo*. Retrieved January 21, 2024, from https://ethicalgeo.org/locus-charter/.

7 United Nations, Committee of Experts on the Global Geospatial Information Management (2012). Consideration of a statement of ethics. *UNGGIM*. Retrieved January 12, 2024, from http://ggim.un.org/meetings/GGIM-committee/documents/GGIM2/E-C20-2012-6%20Statement%20of%20Ethics%20Draft%20Report%205%20July.pdf.

8 Blackemore, M., & Longhorn, R. (2004). *Ethics and GIS: The practitioner's Dilemma*. Retrieved January 12, 2024, from www.iapad.org/wp-content/uploads/2015/07/gis_ethics.pdf.

9 Sinton, D. (2017, June 14). What makes 'do no harm' extra difficult in the geospatial world today? *Directions Magazine*. Retrieved January 12, 2024, from www.directionsmag.com/article/1075.

role in the pandemic in contact tracing and location tracking as well as to monitor compliance with lockdown policies. However, the use of this information also raised important ethical questions about privacy and the responsible use of personal data.[10]

Ethical Issues in Geospatial Information Management

There are a wide range of ethical issues that arise in connection with geospatial technology and information. These issues cut across a number of topics, many of which overlap with legal considerations. For example:

Privacy – Ethical issues associated with location privacy include tracking an individual's location without their informed consent and (ii) sharing location information properly collected for one purpose with third parties to be used for another purposes without the individual's approval.

Data Quality – There are ethical considerations when the quality of geospatial information is misrepresented, particularly when being used for real-time decision-making involving safety or health, and when geospatial information is incomplete or outdated.

Intellectual Property Rights – Ethical issues can arise when geospatial information is used for an unauthorized purpose or without proper attribution. For example, even if web scraping is legal under U.S. law, it raises significant ethical concerns. Similarly, there are also ethical issues when using geospatial information to exploit cultural heritage.

Bias and Discrimination – Poor quality geospatial information can result in unequal distribution of resources and services. Geospatial information can also be used in profiling or result in discrimination based on race, religion, or ethnicity. Each of these raise ethical issues for geospatial professionals.

Ethical issues involving geospatial technology or information arise on a regular basis. Examples include

- auto lenders requiring borrowers to allow the lender to track the vehicles via GPS[11]
- a police department subsidizing private citizens to install ring cameras to help solve crimes[12]

10 Gray, S. (2020, March 25). A closer look at location data: Privacy and pandemics. *Future of Privacy Forum*. Retrieved January 12, 2024, from https://fpf.org/blog/a-closer-look-at-location-data-privacy-and-pandemics/.

11 See WorldGPS. (n.d.). *How GPS tracking technology is improving auto financel*. Retrieved January 12, 2024, from www.seeworldgps.com/knowledge/how-gps-tracking-technology-is-improving-auto-finance/ www.seeworldgps.com/knowledge/how-gps-tracking-technology-is-improving-auto-finance/. Accessed January 12, 2024.

12 WBALTV. (2023, June 19). New Baltimore City program gives rebates on doorbell cameras to help solve crime. *WBALTV*. Retrieved January 11, 2023, from www.wbaltv.com/article/baltimore-city-doorbell-camera-rebate-police-crime-solve/44228511

- a global technology company redrawing borders on a website depending upon the country a visitor is located[13]
- a university changing the name of a country on its map from Taiwan to "Taipei and environs"[14]

These issues are becoming more important as access to geospatial information has increased due to advances in technology, which has made it easier to collect, store, and distribute information on a large scale. It is much harder to protect privacy and intellectual property rights in a world where information is widely available, accessible, and shareable. The ease of collection and use has also made it easier for non-geospatial professionals to collect and use geospatial information without sufficient knowledge of its capabilities and limitations.

Applications of Ethical Theories in Geospatial Intelligence

Three common ethical frameworks that can be applied to geospatial technology are deontology, consequentialism, and virtue ethics.

Deontology is an ethical framework that emphasizes the importance of rules and duties in ethical decision-making rather than the outcomes.[15] For example, deontologists might argue that individuals have a moral duty to protect the privacy and security of others, even if this means limiting access to geospatial information. This might include limiting the access to geospatial information that could be used to identify an individual regardless of the benefits that may be derived.

Consequentialism is an ethical framework that emphasizes the importance of consequences in ethical decision-making.[16] With respect to geospatial information, consequentialism might argue that access to geospatial information should be made broadly available if it results in a significant societal good. For example, a consequential approach during a disaster might advocate that geospatial information be made publicly available to prevent or respond to a natural disaster, even if this resulted in potentially violating the privacy of some individuals.

13 Bensinger, G. (2020, February 14). Google redraws the borders on maps depending on who's looking. *Washington Post*. Retrieved January 11, 2024, from www.washingtonpost.com/technology/2020/02/14/google-maps-political-borders/.

14 Allen-Ebrahimian, B. (2020, March 10). Johns Hopkins coronavirus map changes "Taiwan" to "Taipei and environs". *Axios*. Retrieved January 12, 2024, from www.axios.com/2020/03/10/johns-hopkins-coronavirus-map-taiwan-china.

15 Deontology. (n.d.). *In Britannica*. Retrieved January 12, 2024, from www.britannica.com/topic/deontological-ethics.

16 Consequentalism. (n.d.). *In Britannica*. Retrieved January 12, 2024, from www.britannica.com/topic/consequentialism.

Virtue ethics emphasizes the importance of character and habits in ethical decision-making.[17] Virtue ethics might argue that access should be granted to geospatial information provided it aligns with the principles of fairness, compassion, and respect. For example, a virtue ethical approach to access to geospatial information, taking into account the negative impact that broad access may have on individuals and communities, might limit access to geospatial information to those who need it to make informed decisions.

As technology continues to advance at a rapid pace, there is an increased need for discussion around ethics and geospatial information. The use of artificial intelligence, for example, raises important ethical considerations about the impact of algorithms that make decisions with potential significant impacts to individuals and society.

Challenges in Applying Ethics to the Geospatial Community

One of the main challenges in developing a code of ethics for geospatial professionals is that the geospatial ecosystem is broad. This makes it difficult to develop a code of ethics that can be universally applied. For example, the ethical issues faced by a software engineer in Singapore are very different than those faced by a drone operator in the Middle East or a surveyor in Europe. Similarly, government employees often have different ethical considerations than those in private industry.

Moreover, there are a growing number of stakeholders that are collecting or using geospatial information who do not consider themselves part of the geospatial community. For example, organizations and individuals who work in the autonomous vehicle industry, or with artificial intelligence. They are not likely to abide by a geospatial code of ethics. In fact, some will adopt other distinct codes of ethics, such as for artificial intelligence. In fact, as new segments of the geospatial community develop, they may not even be aware of the existing codes.

It also is important to note that ethical behavior is not synonymous with legal compliance. For example, laws can be inadequate or not up-to-date, and what is considered legal in one country may not be allowed in another. Additionally, laws may not cover all aspects of an ethical issue, or it may not take into consideration the full range of implications of a particular action or decision. On the other hand, an ethical framework is not binding. As such, there would be no way to legally enforce the contents of the framework and limited means to encourage adherence.

An ethical issue becomes a legal issue when a particular action or behavior is prohibited by law. Laws and regulations are put in place to protect certain rights and interests, and when those rights or interests are violated,

17 Virtue ethics. (n.d.). *In Britannica*. Retrieved January 12, 2024, from www.britannica.com/topic/virtue-ethics.

the responsible party can be held liable. For example, if a company is found to be collecting location information without consent, it could be considered an ethical violation of privacy. However, it could also be a legal violation of a data protection law discussed in Chapter 3. Similarly, if a company uses discriminatory algorithms to make decisions affecting individuals, it could be considered unethical and discriminatory. However, it could also be a legal violation of anti-discrimination laws such as the Civil Rights Act.

A focus on ethics can also take away from some of the important discussions that need to be taking place in the geospatial community on the developing legal frameworks that impact geospatial information management. For example, geospatial organizations that are examining location privacy from an ethical standpoint instead of a legal perspective are not engaging with communities that are developing data protection laws. This is unfortunate since the geospatial community is best suited to identify the unique attributes of geospatial information to be considered when developing such laws.

Conclusion

Nongovernmental instruments play an important role in geospatial information management. They have several benefits over laws and regulations. However, because they are nonbinding, they also have limitations. The geospatial community has embraced the role of ethics. However, it should not focus on ethics at the expense of understanding the impact that laws and regulations are having on geospatial information management.

9 Selling Geospatial Products and Services to the U.S. Government

Introduction

The U.S. government is a major buyer of commercial geospatial information products and services. For example, the Department of Defense (DoD) (e.g., the National Geospatial-Intelligence Agency (NGA), the National Reconnaissance Office (NRO) and the combatant commands) acquires significant amounts of geospatial information. In addition, civil agencies such as the National Aeronautics and Space Administration (NASA), the National Oceanic and Atmospheric Administration (NOAA), and the Department of Interior are also significant consumers. This chapter will discuss the differences between commercial transactions and federal procurement. It will also highlight significant legal and policy issues that impact the procurement of geospatial products and services by the U.S. government.

Selling Geospatial Information Products and Services to the U.S. Government

Any discussion of the purchase of products and services by the U.S. government must begin with an understanding of government contracting vehicles. It is also important to understand the difference between sales to the U.S. government and commercial sales. One of the most significant differences is that most federal contracts are subject to the Federal Acquisition Regulation (FAR), as well as any agency-specific FAR supplements. The terms of the FAR are often very different from standard commercial terms.

Standard Types of Government Contracts

The FAR outlines several different contract vehicles that U.S. government agencies may use to procure products and services.[1] Each has its own benefits and risks. The types of contracts most commonly used are as follows:

- *Fixed-Price* – Under a fixed-price contract, a contractor agrees to complete the work for a fixed price.

1 *See* 48 C.F.R. Ch. 1, Subch. C, Pt. 16.

DOI: 10.4324/9781003329961-9

- *Cost-Plus Reimbursement* – Under a cost-plus reimbursement contract, a contractor is paid for the allowed expenses, plus an additional amount for profit.
- *Time and Materials (T&M)* – Under a T&M contract, a contractor charges specified fixed hourly rates (to include wages, overhead, general, and administrative expenses) and a profit for each labor category.

Negotiating contracts with a government agency can be time-consuming and complex. To streamline the government procurement process for certain types of products and services, the U.S. government created the General Services Administration (GSA) Schedule. The GSA Schedule allows federal agencies to purchase goods and services from pre-approved vendors. Companies that have been awarded a GSA Schedule contract have agreed to specific terms and conditions. They have also provided pricing information for their products and services. This allows federal agencies to purchase at pre-negotiated prices without having to go through the lengthy full and open competition.

In 2016, to address changes in the commercial satellite imaging industry and the U.S. government's increasing demand for geospatial information, Special Item Number 541370GEO was added to the GSA Schedule 70. Special Item Number 541370GEO is a blanket purchase order for all Earth observation products, services, and solutions. There were several reasons for creating the category for geospatial information. These include (i) increased visibility and rapid access to commercially available imagery, data, services, and capabilities and (ii) flexibility to adapt to changing markets and vendors.

Special Item Number 541370GEO covers a wide range of geospatial information products and services, including the following:

Advanced data analytics	Predictive analytics
Change detection	Remote sensing and analytical software products
Crowdsourcing	Sensor data (electro-optical, synthetic aperture radar, hyperspectral; geomagnetic field, gravity field; thermal; sonar)
Delivery to ground and mobile ground terminals	Other current and emerging technologies
Direct access service to cell phones, ships, aircraft	Mosaics
Geospatial products and services	Machine learning
Imagery	

However, a business must meet specific eligibility standards to sell geospatial products and services on the GSA Schedule. These requirements include

- being in business for at least two years
- having a record of successful past performance
- the listed product (or service) must be commercially available

In addition, the price that a company charges on the GSA Schedule must be "fair and reasonable." GSA determines whether a price is fair and reasonable based on several factors, including (i) what others are offering for similar products and services, (ii) what the company charges its most favored customer(s), and (iii) historical pricing.

Federal Acquisition Regulation

The FAR is a set of rules and guidelines that govern the acquisition of goods and services by the federal government.[2] The purpose of the FAR is to ensure that the U.S. government's procurement of goods and services is fair and open.

Acquisitions of geospatial technology and information are subject to numerous FAR provisions. For example, under the FAR, computer software includes executable code, source code, code listings, design details, processes, flow charts, and related material that would enable the software to be reproduced, recreated, or recompiled, but it excludes computer databases and computer software documentation.[3] Technical data is defined as "any recorded information of a scientific or technical nature (e.g., product design or maintenance data, computer databases, and computer software documentation)."[4]

Generally, for both noncommercial software and data, the U.S. government's rights depend on the role of government funding in the creation of the software or data:

- *Solely Government Funds* – If the software or technical data is created exclusively from government funds, the U.S. government generally receives unlimited rights. "Unlimited rights" means that the U.S. government can use, modify, reproduce, release, or disclose technical data or computer software in whole or in part, in any manner, and for any purpose whatsoever, and to authorize others to do so.[5]
- *Mixed Funding* – If the software or technical data is created using a combination of private funds and government funds, the FAR provides that the government receives "government purpose rights."[6] Government purpose rights are defined as the right to "use, modify, reproduce, release, or disclose the technical data or computer software within the Government without restriction and outside the Government for a Government purpose." "Government purpose" includes any activity in which the U.S. government is a party, including cooperative agreements with international or

2 Federal Acquisition Regulations § 52.227–14a Rights in Data-General.
3 Federal Acquisition Regulations § 52.227–14a Rights in Data-General.
4 Federal Acquisition Regulations § 52.227–14a Rights in Data-General.
5 Federal Acquisition Regulations § 52.227–14b Rights in Data-General.
6 Federal Acquisition Regulations § 52.227–14b Rights in Data-General.

multinational defense organizations or sales or transfers by the U.S. government to foreign governments or international organizations. Unless the parties negotiate otherwise, a government purpose license remains in effect for five (5) years, after which the government receives "unlimited rights."

- *Solely Private Funds* – If only private funds are used in the creation, then the FAR provides that the government receives restricted rights for software and limited rights for data.[7] "Restricted rights" mean the government's rights to use a computer program with one computer at one time; transfer a computer program to another government agency without permission of the contractor if the transferor destroys all copies of the program and related computer documentation; make the minimum number of copies of computer software required for safekeeping (archive), backup, or modification purposes; modify computer software; and permit contractors or subcontractors performing services in support of a contract to use computer software for correcting deficiencies. "Limited rights" mean the right to use, modify, reproduce, release, perform, display, or disclose technical data, in whole or in part, within the government.

It is crucial for a geospatial professional to properly designate the applicable intellectual property rights the U.S. government is to receive. Failing to do so may result in the government receiving unlimited rights in the software or data.

With respect to patents, a geospatial company that develops a "subject invention" using U.S. government funding must comply with several legal requirements to protect its intellectual property rights.[8] A subject invention is defined as "any invention of the contractor conceived or first actually reduced to practice in the performance of work under a funding agreement."[9] The statutory requirements include timely

- disclosure of the invention to the funding agency
- written election to retain the title of the invention
- filing an initial patent application on the invention[10]

Failure to comply can result in the U.S. government taking ownership of the patent.[11]

The FAR also addresses U.S. government rights in commercial software and data.[12] If permitted under a contract, a geospatial organization can license its geospatial information to the U.S. government under a commercial

7 Federal Acquisition Regulations § 52.227–14b Rights in Data-General.
8 Bayh-Dole Act, 35 U.S.C. §§ 200–212 (1980).
9 48 C.F.R. § 252.
10 35 USC. § 202.
11 See, e.g., *Campbell Plastics Engineering & Mfg., Inc. v. Brownlee*, 389 F.3d 1243 (Fed. Cir. 2004).
12 See FAR 12.211 (Technical Data) and FAR 12.212 (Computer Software).

license. However, several FAR requirements will still apply, such as the choice of law and indemnification limitations.

Pursuant to the OPEN Government Data Act, part of the Foundation for Evidence-Based Policy Making Act, the U.S. government strongly encourages government agencies to obtain data from commercial companies with broad reuse and redistribution rights.[13] As discussed elsewhere in this book, granting open licenses for geospatial information pose challenges for commercial enterprises that wish to limit reuse and distribution of geospatial information, as their business plans may include selling to other government agencies instead of having the U.S. government freely distribute the data.

FAR Supplements

Several government agencies have issued supplements to the FAR. An agency's supplement should be read in conjunction with the FAR as it may impose additional requirements on a contractor. Most notable for geospatial companies are the supplements published by DoD[14] NASA,[15] and the Department of Interior.

The Defense Federal Acquisition Regulations Supplement (DFARS) covers a wide range of topics, including procurement planning, contract types, source selection, contract administration, and small business programs. Some key elements of the DFARS include special provisions for procurement of goods and services critical to national security and reporting requirements for cybersecurity incidents.

Similarly, the NASA Supplemental Federal Acquisition Regulation (NFS) provides additional guidance specific to NASA's procurement activities. The Department of Interior Acquisition Regulation provides additional guidance and clarification on procurement regulations specific to agencies such as the Bureau of Land Management, National Park Service, Fish and Wildlife Service, and Bureau of Indian Affairs.

Special Programs

As government procurement is time-consuming and complicated, the process often defaults to traditional federal contractors, particularly in the defense sector. Due to concerns that these contractors may not provide the innovation, flexibility, and agility needed to face today's challenges, Congress and government agencies have attempted to develop alternative means for non-traditional contractors to participate.

13 Open Licenses. (2022). *Federal enterprise data resources.* Retrieved April 10, 2023, from https://resources.data.gov/open-licenses/.

14 48 CFR.Ch. 2.

15 48 CFR. Ch. 18.

Other Transactions (OTs)

Other Transaction Agreements (OTAs) are a type of contract used by the federal government to acquire goods and services not typically procured through traditional procurement methods and are not subject to many FAR provisions. This allows for more flexibility and innovation. They are often formed between the government and non-traditional contractors, including small businesses and universities. OTAs are generally used for early-stage research and development projects with a high degree of technical risk.

The Small Business Innovation Research and Small Business Technology Transfer Programs[16]

The Small Business Innovation Research (SBIR) and Small Business Technology Transfer (STTR) programs are designed to encourage domestic small businesses to engage in research and development with the potential for commercialization. These programs allow small businesses to explore applications of their technology as well as commercialization opportunities. A number of government agencies, including the U.S. Air Force, Space Force, and NASA, have SBIR/STTR programs of interest to geospatial companies.[17]

The SBIR Program has three phases:[18] Phase I establishes the technical merit, feasibility, and commercial potential of the proposed R&D efforts. It gives the awardee a chance to prove the quality of its work prior to providing further Phase II support. Phase I awards are generally between $50,000 and $275,000 and last for up to six months (SBIR) or one year (STTR).

Phase II contracts continue the research and development efforts initiated in Phase I. Funding is based on (i) the results achieved in Phase I and (ii) the merits and potential of the proposed Phase II project. Typically, only Phase I awardees are eligible for a Phase II award. Phase II awards are generally for two years and $750,000.

A Phase III award allows the awardee to pursue commercialization of the technology developed under previous awards. However, funding for Phase III must come from federal agencies.

Grants and Cooperative Agreements

The Federal Grant and Cooperative Agreement Act (FGCA)[19] gives government agencies the authority to establish grants and enter into cooperative

16 15 U.S.C. § 638.

17 See, e.g., SBIR Ignite. (2022). *NASA*. Retrieved July 23, 2022, from https://sbir.nasa.gov/ignite.

18 See, e.g., Small Business Administration. (2020, October). *Small Business Innovation Research (SBIR) and Small Business Technology Transfer (STTR) Program.*

19 31 USC Ch. 63.

agreements for certain activities. There are significant differences between a grant and a cooperative agreement from a funding standpoint. Under a grant a federal agency will provide the company funding. However, under a cooperative agreement, while the agency will be substantially involved in the agreed upon activity, it does not provide funding to the recipient.

Cooperative Research and Development Agreements (CRADAs) are a vehicle often used between the U.S. government and the geospatial community. CRADAs involve one (or more) federal agencies and a private-sector organization, such as a company or university, jointly conducting research and development (R&D) activities. CRADAs enable a federal agency to leverage the expertise, resources, and facilities of the private-sector organization to advance its mission while also providing the private-sector organization with access to the agency's equipment, facilities, data, etc., They are often used by government agencies to conduct R&D in areas specific to the agency's mission, such as defense or space. All parties to the CRADA share the costs, risks, and benefits of the R&D activities. The specific terms of the CRADA, such as the length of the agreement, the scope of the R&D activities, and the sharing of costs and intellectual property rights, are set forth in an agreement.

While navigating the federal procurement laws to sell any type of product or service to the U.S. government may be difficult, selling geospatial information and related products and services is particularly challenging.

U.S. Government Procurement of Commercial Satellite Remote Sensing Imagery

The U.S. government has repeatedly stated its goal is to support the U.S. commercial satellite remote sensing industry. For example, the 2003 U.S. Commercial Remote Sensing Policy stated that the U.S. should "rely to the maximum practical extent on U.S. commercial sensing space capabilities for filling imagery and geospatial needs for military, intelligence, foreign policy, homeland security, and civil users."[20] This outward support for the commercial satellite imagery industry has continued through several administrations. Most recently, the 2020 U.S. National Space Policy stated,

> [T]he Secretary of Commerce shall license and regulate private remote sensing systems consistent with the recognition that long-term United States national security and foreign policy interests are best served by ensuring that United States industry continues to lead the rapidly maturing and highly competitive commercial space-based remote sensing market.[21]

20 US Commercial Remote Sensing Policy. (2003, April). *National security presidential directives*. Retrieved July 31, 2022, from https://irp.fas.org/offdocs/nspd/remsens.html.

21 US National Space Policy. (2020). *US National Space Policy*. Retrieved July 30, 2022, from https://trumpwhitehouse.archives.gov/wp-content/uploads/2020/12/National-Space-Policy.pdf.

In 2021, government support for U.S. commercial satellite remote sensing became law as Title 10, Subtitle A, Part I, Chapter 22, Subchapter I: Missions and Authority of the U.S. Code was amended to state,

> In acquiring geospatial intelligence, the Secretary of Defense and the Director of National Intelligence, in coordination with the Director of the National Reconnaissance Office and the Director of the National Geospatial-Intelligence Agency, shall leverage, to the extent practicable, the capabilities of the industry of the United States, including through the use of domestic commercial geospatial-intelligence services and acquisition of domestic commercial satellite imagery.[22]

Under the law, the NRO and NGA are required to consider commercial capabilities as part of an analysis of alternatives for the future acquisition of geospatial information. If they determine there is a cost-effective domestic commercial capability or service available that can meet the DoD's or Intelligence Community's geospatial information requirements, preference should be given to using such domestic commercial capability or service.

Civil agencies have received similar direction from Congress to explore procuring commercial satellite imagery to fulfill their respective missions. For example, in an Explanatory Statement which accompanied the Omnibus Appropriations Act 2009, Congress requested a report from NOAA on its plans to obtain data from commercial sources.[23] Subsequently, the Consolidated Appropriations Act, 2010 directed NOAA to report to Congress on how the agency could benefit from acquiring commercial space-based data and its plans to obtain such data.[24]

The use of commercial satellite imagery by civil agencies was also referenced in the 2020 National Space Policy. It directed NASA, and the Departments of Commerce and Defense to collaborate with the private sector and international partners to ensure continued collection of global meteorological and environmental satellite data. Such acquisitions are meant to be cost-effective and resilient, to include procurement of commercial data. NOAA developed its Commercial Space Policy, which addresses NOAA's various interactions with the commercial sector (i.e., hosted payloads, rideshares, launches, and data buys).[25] The policy describes several actions that NOAA

22 (Pub. L. No. 116–283, div. A, title XVI, §1612, Jan. 1, 2021, 134 Stat. 4049, as amended by Pub. L. 117–81, div. A, title XVI, §1606, Dec. 27, 2021, 135 Stat. 2079).

23 P.L. 111–8: Omnibus Appropriations Act, 2009, Pub. L. No. 111–8, 123 Stat. 524 (2009).

24 P.L. 111–117: Consolidated Appropriations Act, 2010, Pub. L. No. 111–117, 123 Stat. 3035.

25 National Oceanic and Atmospheric Administration. (2016). *NAO 217–109: NOAA commercial space policy*. Retrieved January 21, 2024, from www.noaa.gov/organization/administration/nao-217-109-noaa-commercial-space-policy.

plans to take to acquire data or data products from commercial satellite providers. These include

- working with industry to evaluate and implement business models and legal mechanisms that allow NOAA priorities and requirements to be met with commercial capabilities
- exploring demonstration projects to validate the viability of assimilating commercially provided environmental data and data products into NOAA meteorological models
- periodically publishing NOAA mission requirements and capability gaps that offer appropriate opportunities for the purchase and use of commercial space capabilities and services
- periodically evaluating commercially available space capabilities and services that could potentially address NOAA mission requirements

Congress has also directed NASA to work more closely with the commercial remote sensing industry. For example, Section 51 U.S.C. § 60302 directs NASA to develop a sustained relationship with the U.S. commercial remote sensing industry and to rely, subject to applicable laws and policies, on industries services to the maximum practicable extent. It also directs NASA to collaborate with the private sector in the U.S. to identify Earth science applications prototypes to enhance the use of both government and commercial geospatial information to improve decision-making.

In response to these and other directives, U.S. government agencies have established several lines of effort. Since 2002, the U.S. government, through NGA and the NRO, have entered into a series of large contracts with U.S. commercial satellite imagery providers to acquire commercial data products and services. For example, in 2003 NGA entered into agreements with three U.S. commercial imagery providers to purchase up to $500 million in data and data products.[26] In 2018 NGA updated its Commercial GEOINT strategy, with a purpose to "embrace new suppliers and services by working with our intelligence community (IC), combatant commands, military services, and federal civil partners to employ the best mix of commercial and national sources in order to secure strategic competitive advantage and outpace our adversaries."[27] More recently, in 2022, the NRO entered into multi-year contracts with three commercial satellite imagery providers that

26 Office of Space Commerce. (2004). *NGA Awards nextview remote sensing data buys.* Retrieved January 21, 2024, from www.space.commerce.gov/nga-awards-nextview-remote-sensing-data-buys/.

27 National Geospatial-Intelligence Agency. (2018). *Commercial GEOINT Strategy: 2018 update.* Retrieved January 28, 2024 from.

could result in the procurement of up to $4 billion dollars of data and data products.[28]

These large procurements have focused on electro-optical imagery data and associated products. However, the NRO has also entered into smaller contracts for other phenomenologies. For example, in 2022 the NRO announced that it had awarded study contracts for commercial radar capabilities.[29] Subsequently, in 2023 it awarded study contracts to companies offering hyperspectral capabilities.[30]

On the civil side, in December 2017, NASA's Earth Science Division (ESD) launched the Commercial Smallsat Data Acquisition (CSDA) Program Pilot, also known as the Private-Sector Small Constellation Satellite Data Product Pilot. The aim of the pilot was to identify, evaluate, and acquire remote sensing imagery and data to support NASA's Earth science research and application activities. Following successful implementation of the pilot, CSDA was established as a program, under which several contracts have been awarded.[31]

Similarly, NOAA works with the commercial sector through its Commercial Data Program (the "CDP"). For example, the Commercial Weather Data Pilot (CWDP) is used to demonstrate the quality and impact of commercial data on weather forecast models while the Commercial Data Purchase supports operational weather forecasting.[32]

However, as detailed in two U.S. government reports, there are roadblocks in both the defense and civil procurement of commercial satellite remote sensing products.[33] Many of these roadblocks are purely technical or operational. For example, the NOAA policy is that it will "apply the same validation, data

28 Hitchens, T. (2023, May 23). Breaking defense NRO seeking new electro-optical imagery from private sector. *Breaking Defense*. Retrieved January 21, 2024 from https://breakingdefense.com/2023/05/nro-seeking-new-electro-optical-imagery-from-private-sector/.

29 National Reconnaissance Office. (2022). *BAA Award press release CSPO*. Retrieved January 12, 2024, fromwww.nro.gov/Portals/65/documents/news/press/2022/BAA_Award_Press_Release_CSPO_20220119.pdf.

30 National Reconnaissance Office. (2023). *HSI study contracts press release*. Retrieved January 12, 2024, from www.nro.gov/Portals/135/documents/news/press/2023/HSI_Study_Contracts_Press_Release_FINAL.pdf?ver=SK9FqMYjMRwl8cRsIgMWaA%3D%3D.

31 National Aeronautics and Aviation Administration. (2023). *NASA selects commercial smallsat data acquisition contractors*. Retrieved January 28, 2024, from www.nasa.gov/news-release/nasa-selects-commercial-smallsat-data-acquisition-contractors/.

32 Office of Space Commerce. (2023). *OAA Awards contract for ocean surface winds data pilot*. Retrieved January 12, 2024, from www.space.commerce.gov/noaa-awards-contract-for-ocean-surface-winds-data-pilot/.

33 As discussed further in the next section, the GAO report "National Security Space: Actions Needed to Better Use Commercial Satellite Imagery and Analytics" details how adoption of commercial satellite imagery within the DoD and Intelligence Communities has been slow. Similarly, a report by the Subcommittee on U.S. Group on Earth Observations Committee on the Environment of the National Science and Technology Council highlights the challenges of integrating commercial date into the U.S. Government EO Enterprise.

integrity, and security criteria to commercial data and data products as those obtained by other means, before entering into any binding agreement for the purchase and utilization of observations to support the NOAA mission."[34] From an operational standpoint, the government's requirements-based process for procuring imagery products and services is also hindering broader adoption. As noted in a 2023 Government Accountability Office (GAO) report, "Space Force officials also emphasized that the current requirements approach for acquiring commercial imagery is not dynamic enough to leverage industry innovation that could address warfighter needs."[35]

Similarly,

> NGA also faces challenges integrating data from emerging capabilities acquired by NRO[36], according to NGA officials. For example, NGA officials reported that, although NRO has a number of study contracts exploring commercial radar capabilities, NGA does not have formal requirements to ingest and process this commercial radar data in their ground systems from these emerging capabilities. NGA can use commercial radar data to a limited degree, but the agency has no sustainable capability or means to scale up the use of this satellite radar data at the enterprise level, according to agency officials.[37]

This requirements-focused procurement process has a significant impact on the commercial sector. For example, pursuant to the FAR, Broad Agency Announcements are intended to focus on basic research and exploration, not for system development or procuring hardware.[38] According to the GAO report "NRO officials did not identify a separate process – one that could avoid a potentially lengthy requirements-related process – for transitioning contracts associated with the Broad Agency Announcement to operational

34 National Oceanic and Atmospheric Administration. (2016). *NAO 217–109: NOAA commercial space policy*. Retrieved January 21, 2024 from www.noaa.gov/organization/administration/nao-217-109-noaa-commercial-space-policy

35 U.S. Government Accountability Office. (2022). *National security space: Actions needed to better use commercial satellite imagery and analytics (GAO-22–106106)*. Retrieved January 21, 2024, from www.gao.gov/assets/gao-22-106106.pdf.

36 Given the nature of the responsibilities, the relationship between NRO and NGA can be complicated. This is shown by the history of the data buys of commercial imagery. Until 2017, NGA was responsible for buying all commercial geospatial intelligence-related imagery and data. In 2017 the Trump administration shifted the authority for purchase of satellite imagery to the NRO, with NGA retaining authority over acquisition of all non-satellite imagery.

37 U.S. Government Accountability Office. (2022). *National security space: Actions needed to better use commercial satellite imagery and analytics (GAO-22–106106)*. Retrieved January 21, 2024 from www.gao.gov/assets/gao-22-106106.pdf.

38 Federal Acquisition Regulation 35.016 Broad agency announcement.

ones."[39] Similarly, the GAO report noted that "while the NRO had awarded five study contracts as of July 2021 it has transitioned only one commercial vendor from a study contract to an operational support contract."[40]

Legal and policy issues are also contributing to procurement challenges as well. These include preference for entities considered to be U.S. companies, under the Buy American Act and associated government-wide and agency policies, covered in more detail in Chapter 6. Another contributing factor are the legal and policy requirements imposed on government agencies to pertaining to open data.

The Impact of U.S. Open Data Laws and Policies

On the civil side, there is an inherent conflict between "open data" and the business models of commercial satellite companies. As described in further detail in Chapter 10, the U.S. government has pushed for data from non-classified satellite systems to be "open." For example, in 2008, the U.S. government provided free and open access to the archive of Landsat imagery. In 2009, under then President Obama, the U.S. government began an initiative to make government data across all agencies more open and available. Subsequently, the Office of Management and Budget (OMB) published the Open Data Policy – Managing Information as an Asset.[41] The OMB policy requires federal agencies to apply open licenses to their data. However, it also provides that agencies should procure data from the private sector with terms that make the data broadly available. Specifically, the policy states,

> [W]hen information is acquired or accessed by an agency through performance of a contract, appropriate existing clauses shall be utilized to meet these [Open Data] objectives while recognizing that contractors may have proprietary interests in such information, and that protection of such information may be necessary to encourage qualified contractors to participate in and apply innovative concepts to government programs.[42]

The OPEN Government Data Act was signed into law as part of the Foundations for Evidence-Based Policymaking Act of 2018.[10] It requires agencies to

39 U.S. Government Accountability Office. (2022). *National security space: Actions needed to better use commercial satellite imagery and analytics (GAO-22–106106)*. Retrieved January 21, 2024, from www.gao.gov/assets/gao-22-106106.pdf.

40 Id.

41 Office of Management and Budget. (2013). *Open data policy–Managing information as an asset (M-13–13)*. Retrieved January 12, 2024, from https://obamawhitehouse.archives.gov/sites/default/files/omb/memoranda/2013/m-13-13.pdf.

42 Office of Management and Budget. (2013). *Open data policy–Managing information as an asset (M-13–13)*. Retrieved January 12, 2024, from https://obamawhitehouse.archives.gov/sites/default/files/omb/memoranda/2013/m-13-13.pdf.

"make each public data asset of [their agency] available as an open Government data asset; and available under an open license."[43]

The issue of licensing becomes even more complex for government agencies due to the data rights set forth in the FAR. Geospatial information does not fit easily into the definition of "technical data." For example, according to a an Office of Science and Technology Policy (OSTP) report (the "OSTP Report), "[t]here are some outstanding issues between the agencies about whether a geospatial information set itself constitutes 'technical data' or 'computer software' under the relevant FAR."[44]

Moreover, government agencies may procure data via several different means. The applicability of the FAR may differ depending on, for example, whether the procurement was through direct commodity purchase or direct services collection. The OSTP Report highlights,

> This issue is complex. Each data procurement may have valid reasons to resolve procurements differently. For example, if an agency is seeking data from a provider that is collecting the data routinely and offering the data commercially to multiple entities, it may be appropriate to consider a procurement with a EULA, rather than issuing data rights clauses for the products. FAR Part 27 would not be applicable to the license terms where the EULAs are applicable to but not to the data rights clause for the purpose of a contract, whereas the EULAs provision contained in the contractor's standard commercial license or government EULAs would not be contrary to the clauses. For example, if an agency is seeking collection of specific data that were not collected commercially, the data rights may be procured under a EULA, with additional charges for withholding rights or by implementing the data rights clauses that may be more appropriate, allowing all data rights to the agency (as opposed to the data provider retaining ownership and offering a license to the agency). Agencies should be cognizant of what type of contract they are offering when determining which data rights or licensing are appropriate for each acquisition.[45]

As a result, when procuring commercial geospatial information, government agencies must balance the FAR, open data policies as well as the terms of

43 44 U.S. Code § 3506–Federal agency responsibilities.

44 Office of Science and Technology Policy (OSTP). (2022, July). *United States government commercial earth observations data purchases: perspectives from the earth observations enterprise.* Retrieved January 21, 2024 from https://earthdata.nasa.gov/esds/csdap.

45 Office of Science and Technology Policy (OSTP). (2022, July). *United States government commercial earth observations data purchases: perspectives from the earth observations enterprise.* Retrieved January 21, 2024, from https://earthdata.nasa.gov/esds/csdap.

commercial licenses. This can make the procurement process for geospatial information complex, particularly for civil agencies.[46]

For example, NOAA's Commercial Space Policy touches upon many of these licensing issues. It states that NOAA will

- seek to maximize the public benefit of environmental data and data products acquired through commercial space solutions by negotiating the least restrictive terms of use possible
- consider the impact of acquiring commercial data or data products on other Federal agencies, international partners, the private weather enterprise, academic and research communities, and other stakeholders
- consider the cost associated with various terms of use of commercial data, and
- evaluate the use of space-based data and data products obtained from commercial providers as well as data sharing agreements on a case-by-case basis

The GEO report highlighted the challenges associated with this licensing complexity:

> Regarding the extent of data sharing rights in any license, there was no consensus between data provider and data users. Many data providers emphasized that licenses, allowing full and open sharing undercut their opportunity to sell to multiple users and create markets.[47]
>
> When over-buying unnecessary rights, more than the program's needs, a single agency conducting the procurement ends up burdening its own funds for other agencies' use of the data. U.S. Government EO agencies will continue to discuss this difference as the government balances fostering commercial enterprises (e.g., Weather Enterprise) and the perception the government is buying data that someone could resell.

In an effort to align licensing terms to make it easier for both government agencies and the commercial sector, the NRO adopted a series of standard commercial license agreements with different licensing terms.[48] NASA adopted the NRO-developed family of license agreements to enable broad levels of dissemination and shareability of commercial data with other

46 Some of the same on DoD, but purchase are so large that commercial providers are OK with it. Also sharing from DoD to other agencies is limited, despite the license.

47 Office of Science and Technology Policy. (2022, July). *United States government commercial earth observations data purchases: Perspectives from the earth observations enterprise.* Retrieved January 21, 2024, from https://earthdata.nasa.gov/esds/csdap 4.

48 Werner, D. (2021, October 8). *Space News NRO establishes licenses and cybersecurity rules for commercial imagery providers.* Retrieved January 21, 2024 from https://spacenews.com/nro-commercial-licensing-cybersecurity/.

agencies and the scientific community. NOAA adopted its own set of licenses, which – while similar – do have material differences. As stated in the OSTP Report, one of the most significant differences between the two is in the use of the term "public use." The NRO licenses define "public use" as retaining industry copyright and prevents use for commercial purposes. NOAA has defined "public use" to mean without any restrictions on use, including commercial use.[49] However, while NOAA ensures third-party users are aware of the licensing restrictions, it tells vendors that NOAA will not be liable for any third-party misuse.[50]

Procurement of Other Types of Geospatial Information

The procurement process for mapping services is also complex. One complexity is the application of the Brooks Act to federal procurement of mapping and surveying services. The Brooks Act, enacted in 1972, established a qualification-based selection (QBS) process for the procurement of architects and engineers for design contracts in federal projects.[51] As a result, the federal government's procurement of services from architects and engineers are based on demonstrated competence and qualification rather than price, which is the case for most government procurements. The rationale for the Brooks Act is that for these services, quality is more important than price, so Congress did not want contracts for design contracts to go to the lowest bidder.

In 1988, the Brooks Act was amended to include surveying and mapping. Specifically, Section 403 of Pub. L. 101–574 (SBA Reauthorization and Amendments Act of 1990) required that "the definition of architectural and engineering services includes surveying and mapping services to which the selection procedures of Subpart FAR 36.6 of the Federal Acquisition Regulation apply."

Subsequently, an issue arose as to whether the amendment to the Brooks Act applied to all surveying and mapping services or simply to those associated with architectural and engineering services. The determination was that the amendment should be read to apply only to those activities related to architectural and engineering services. Consequently, FAR 36.601 was amended to read as follows:

> Professional surveying and mapping services of an architectural or engineering nature. Surveying is considered to be an architectural and engineering service and shall be procured pursuant to section 36.601

49 Office of Science and Technology Policy. (2022, July). *United States government commercial earth observations data purchases: perspectives from the earth observations enterprise.* Retrieved January 21, 2024, from https://earthdata.nasa.gov/esds/csdap.

50 Id.

51 40 USC Ch. 11: Selection of architects and engineers.

> from registered surveyors or architects and engineers. Mapping associated with the research, planning, development, design, construction, or alteration of real property is considered to be an architectural and engineering service and is to be procured pursuant to section 36.601. However, mapping services that are not connected to traditionally understood or accepted architectural and engineering activities, are not incidental to such architectural and engineering activities, or have not in themselves traditionally been considered architectural and engineering services shall be procured pursuant to provisions in parts 13, 14, and 15 (i.e., the competitive bidding process).

Despite this clarification, the application of the Brooks Act to mapping and surveying remained an open issue in federal procurement. For example, Section 8101 of the National Defense Appropriations Act for Fiscal Year 1999 (Pub. L. 262) directed NIMA (the predecessor to NGA), except for services critical to national security, to use the procedures in FAR Subpart 36.6 when using fiscal year 1999 funds to award contracts for mapping, charting, and geodesy activities, rather than the provisions in FAR Parts 13, 14, and 15. Subsequently, the Department of Defense, the General Services Administration, and NASA published a notice in the Federal Register, at the request of the FAR Council, seeking comments on the application of the Brooks Act to mapping services.[52] After public comment, the Defense Acquisition Regulations Council and the Civilian Agency Acquisition Council decided to maintain a distinction between the procurement of surveying and mapping services that were related to architecture and engineering and those that were not.

In 2006, several trade associations sued the federal government, alleging that it was not properly enforcing the Brooks Act with respect to mapping. In 2007, a judge ruled against the trade associations. Although the case was decided on a technical legal matter rather than on the applicability of QBS in the procurement of mapping services, the court noted that the term mapping services was much broader than traditional mapping services conducted by surveyors.

As a result, procurement for surveying and mapping services by the U.S. government varies by government agency. One can debate from a legal standpoint the extent QBS under the Brooks Act should apply to all mapping services procured by the federal government. However, the different procurement practices have increased the complexity of doing business with the U.S. government for geospatial companies wishing to provide services across the federal government.

52 70 FR 20329–20333: Federal Acquisition Regulation; Application of the Brooks Act to Mapping Services; Analysis of Comments, 70 Fed. Reg. 20329 (April 19, 2005).

Conclusion

The U.S. government procures significant amounts of geospatial technology and information from the private sector. Sales to the federal government differ in a number of respects to commercial transactions. Contractors must be aware of both the FAR and any agency-specific supplements. In addition, there are unique issues that arise with respect to the procurement of geospatial information by the U.S. government. These include issues associated with commercial satellite remote sensing data and products, open data, as well as the procurement of mapping and surveying services.

10 Role of Federal Civil Agencies in Geospatial Information Management

Introduction

There is no one government agency within the U.S. responsible for geospatial information management. Rather, many federal agencies, cutting across both the civil and defense/intelligence sectors of the U.S. government play important roles. Each are subject to distinct laws, regulations, and polices that impact their authority and obligations. Some of these laws and policies have a direct impact on geospatial information management, such as the Geospatial Data Act of 2018 and OMB Circular No. A-130. The impacts of others, such as Space Policy Directive 5 (SPD-5), which addresses cybersecurity in space, and Part 107 of the Federal Aviation Administration (FAA) regulations, which pertains to operations of small drones in the U.S. airspace, are more indirect but nevertheless important.

This diffuse governance structure may be expected, given the size and nature of the federal government, the wide range of geospatial technologies used by government agencies, the different types of geospatial information collected and the variety of geospatial-enabled applications and services within the U.S. government. However, this chapter will show how this approach can complicate geospatial information management within the civil sector of the United States. In addition, as numerous government agencies are responsible for collecting geospatial information, effective geospatial information requires sharing among federal agencies as well as with other sectors of the government and the private sector. The issue is further complicated because of, as discussed in earlier chapters, the dual use of many geospatial technologies and applications. As a result, both civil and military/intelligence agencies have vested interests in geospatial information, which can cause conflict and confusion, particularly given the classified nature of some geospatial projects and the legal and policy limitations on military and intelligence agencies to operate on civil matters.

In an effort to make it easier for the reader to understand the authorities and relationships between government agencies, the discussion of geospatial information management within the U.S. government is split into two

DOI: 10.4324/9781003329961-10

chapters. This chapter will focus on the role of civil agencies. Chapter 11 will discuss the role of the defense/intelligence agencies.

However, it is important to remember while reading both chapters that this dichotomy can be somewhat misleading. For example, several federal committees, such as the Federal Geographic Data Committee (FGDC) and the National Executive Committee for Space-Based Positioning, Navigation, and Timing (PNT), are required by law to have representatives from both civil and defense/intelligence agencies. Moreover, there can be significant overlap between civil and defense/intelligence agencies on matters such as geospatial standards. In reviewing these chapters, the reader is encouraged to consider whether the U.S. government's governance structure facilitates or hinders effective geospatial information management.

Role of Civil Agencies

Geospatial Data Act of 2018

The Geospatial Data Act of 2018 (GDA) codified OMB Circular A-16 and other existing policies within the U.S. government. OMB Circular A-16 was originally issued in 1953 to improve the federal government's mapping and surveying efforts. It has been revised several times to address the evolution of geospatial information management. For example, the 1967 revisions outlined the surveying and mapping responsibilities of the Department of the Interior, the Department of Commerce, and the Department of State. In 1990 it was revised to address the digitalization of spatial data. Subsequently in 2002, OMB Circular A-16 was updated again to "reflect the changes that have taken place in geographic information management and technology, and to clearly define agency and FGDC responsibilities," including further defining the components of the National Spatial Data Infrastructure .[1] Subsequently, Executive Order 13286 was issued on February 28, 2003, addressing the role of the newly created Department of Homeland Security in geospatial information management. Supplemental Guidance was issued in 2010, to further define and clarify OMB Circular A-16 in order "to facilitate the adoption and implementation of a coordinated and effective Federal geospatial asset management capability that will improve support of mission-critical business requirements of the Federal Government and its stakeholders."[2]

1 The concept of a National Spatial Data Infrastructure was initially introduced by Executive Order 12906 of April 11, 1994, Coordinating Geographic Data Acquisition and Access: The National Spatial Data Infrastructure. For a discussion of the evolution of OMB Circular A-16, see White House (August 2002) Circular No. A-16 Revised, Retrieved January 27, 2024 from https://obamawhitehouse.archives.gov/omb/circulars_a016_rev/.

2 For a discussion of the evolution of OMB Circular A-16, see Executive Office of the President Office of Management and Budget. (2010, November) Retrieved January 12, 2024, from www.fgdc.gov/policyandplanning/a-16/omb-circular-a16-supplemental-guidance

Although GDA is now the operative law for civil geospatial information management within the United States, it did not make any significant changes in how geospatial information is managed. For example, the GDA does not give the FGDC greater authority over agency budgets for geospatial information management. Instead, it draws heavily from the concepts and structure of OMB Circular A-16 and related policies.

The preamble to the GDA contains several findings of Congress. One such finding was that the private sector has an invaluable role in acquiring and producing geospatial information for the federal government and that this role also contributes to the U.S. economy. Another finding was that greater access and use to geospatial information have spurred economic growth and innovation and numerous civil benefits. Each of these principles can be found in elements of the GDA.

Federal Geographic Data Committee (FGDC)

The FGDC is an interagency committee. It currently consists of over 25 government agencies involved in civil geospatial information management as well as the National Geospatial Intelligence Agency (NGA) and the Department of Homeland Security. The FGDC is chaired by a representative from the Secretary of Interior, and the vice chair is the Director of the Office of Management and Budget (OMB). The FGDC Steering Committee is responsible for providing leadership and direction for the FGDC.[3] In addition, the FGDC has several subcommittees consisting of representatives from federal agencies and recognized stakeholder groups that work on various data themes (e.g., geologic data, addresses, vegetation.)

The GDA outlines a number of high-level responsibilities of the FGDC, many of which involve coordinating with other agencies and departments. These responsibilities include

- defining the roles and responsibilities of and promoting and guiding cooperation and coordination among federal agencies, state, tribal, and local

3 The Steering committee consists of representatives from the Department of the Interior; Office of Management and Budget; Department of Agriculture; Department of Commerce; National Geospatial Intelligence Agency; United States Army Corps of Engineers; Department of Education; Department of Energy; Department of Health and Human Services; Department of Homeland Security; Department of Housing and Urban Development; Department of the Interior; Department of Justice; Department of Labor; Department of State; Department of Transportation; Department of the Treasury; Department of Veterans Affairs; Environmental Protection Agency; Federal Communications Commission; General Services Administration; Library of Congress; National Aeronautics and Space Administration; National Archives and Records Administration; National Capital Planning Commission; National Science Foundation; Nuclear Regulatory Commission; Office of Personnel Management; Small Business Administration; Smithsonian Institution; Tennessee Valley Authority; U.S. Agency for International Development.

governments, universities, and the private sector in the collection, production, sharing, and use of geospatial information and the implementation of the National Spatial Data Infrastructure (NSDI)
- leading the development and management of the NSDI
- designating and overseeing the management of the national data asset themes
- establishing and maintaining geospatial information standards
- reviewing compliance by agencies of geospatial information standards
- ensuring the operations of the GeoPlatform
- fostering communication with and among relevant agencies and other entities and individuals relating to geospatial information management

The GDA also details other aspects of geospatial information management within the U.S. For example, the GDA also codified the GeoPlatform, an effort that the FGDC had been developing for a number of years. The GeoPlatform is "an Internet-based capability providing shared and trusted geospatial data, services, and applications for use by government agencies and partners to meet their mission needs and by the public."[4] Essentially it is intended to be a "one-stop" shop for geospatial data and services. The GDA sets forth several requirements for the GeoPlatform, including accessibility and security. The FGDC chair is responsible for choosing the federal agency responsible for developing and operating the GeoPlatform.

The GDA also directs the FGDC to prepare and maintain a strategic plan for an NSDI, defined in the GDA as "the technology, policies, criteria, standards, and employees necessary to promote geospatial data sharing throughout the Federal, State, Tribal, and local governments, and the private sector (including nonprofit organizations and institutions of higher education)." It also directs the FGDC to advise federal and nonfederal stakeholders (states, tribes, etc.) on their respective roles and responsibilities with respect to the NSDI. The GDA incorporates many of the concepts of Executive Order 12906, issued by then President Clinton in 1994.

As noted in several chapters of this book, standards play an important role in geospatial information management, particularly with regard to data sharing. The FGDC has endorsed several standards pertaining to geospatial information. As a result, it is not surprising that the GDA codified the FGDC's authority to establish standards for data themes.

Civil agencies that collect, produce, acquire, maintain, distribute, use, or preserve geospatial information to fulfill the mission of that agency are

4 Federal Geographic Data Committee, GeoPlatform Frequently Asked Questions, Retrieved January 21, 2024, from www.fgdc.gov/initiatives/geospatial-platform/geoplatform_faq

defined as "covered agencies" in the GDA. The GDA sets forth a comprehensive list of duties for covered agencies, including to

- support the NSDI by preparing, maintaining, publishing, and implementing a strategy for advancing geographic information and related geospatial information and activities appropriate to its mission
- collect, maintain, disseminate, and preserve geospatial information for sharing with other federal agencies and nonfederal users
- promote the integration of geospatial information
- allocate resources for effective geospatial information collection, production, and stewardship with regard to it activities
- use geospatial information standards (including the standards for metadata).
- coordinate and work in partnership with other federal agencies, agencies of state, tribal, and local governments, institutions of higher education, and the private sector
- cost- effectively collect, integrate, maintain, disseminate, and preserve geospatial information, building upon existing nonfederal geospatial information to the extent possible.
- use geospatial information to:
    - make federal geospatial information and services more useful to the public
    - enhance operations
    - support decision-making
    - enhance reporting to the public and to Congress
- protect personal privacy and maintain confidentiality in accordance with federal policy and law
- determine if existing federal, state, local, or private geospatial information meets the needs of the covered agency before expending funds for geospatial information collection
- ensure that a person receiving federal funds for geospatial information collection provides high-quality data
- every two years, conduct an audit of its activities with respect to geospatial information management as well as its compliance with the GDA

Of note, while agencies within the Department of Defense and the Intelligence Community "collect, produce, maintain, distribute, use and preserve" vast amounts of geospatial information, they are excluded from these portions of the GDA.

The GDA authorized the FGDC to identify data themes. The FGDC has currently identified 18 data themes consisting of more than 173 datasets.[5]

5 Federal Geographic Data Committee, A-16 NGDA Portfolio Management, Retrieved January 21, 2024, from www.fgdc.gov/what-we-do/manage-federal-geospatial-resources/a-16-portfolio-management/ngda-themes-and-datasets

The GDA states that agencies designated as a lead agency for a data theme by the FGDC has additional responsibilities. These responsibilities include

- ensuring the coordinated management of the data and related services and products
- providing leadership and facilitating the development and implementation of geospatial information standards
- establishing goals that support the NSDI strategic plan
- incorporating needs of users into the national data theme
- designating a point of contact responsible for developing, maintaining, coordination relating to, and disseminating data using the GeoPlatform

National Geospatial Advisory Committee

The GDA also codifies the National Geospatial Advisory Committee (NGAC), which was established in 2008. Its purpose is to provide advice and recommendations to the Chair of the FGDC. The members of the NGAC are selected by the FGDC Chair and are intended to represent the viewpoints of various stakeholders involved in the geospatial ecosystem, including state and local government, industry, trade associations, academia, and NGOs. The responsibilities of the NGAC under the GDA include

- providing advice and recommendations relating to (i) the management of federal and national geospatial programs, (ii) the development of the NSDI, and (iii) implementation of the GDA
- reviewing and commenting on geospatial policy and management issues
- ensuring the views of representatives of nonfederal interested parties involved in national geospatial activities are conveyed to the FGDC

Department of Interior

The Secretary of the Interior has significant responsibility for geospatial information management in addition to its role as Chair of the FGDC. For example, the Department of Interior is the lead agency for several data themes. It also is responsible for overseeing several Earth observation and mapping programs, including the National Land Imaging Program, which includes the Landsat satellites and the 3D Elevation program.

The Department of Interior's authorities for these roles come from a variety of sources. For example, the United States Geologic Survey (USGS) within the Department of Interior was established by the Organic Act of March 3, 1879, as amended.[6] The Organic Act directed USGS to classify the public lands and examine the geological structure, mineral resources, and products

6 43 U.S.C. 31 et seq.

within and outside the national domain. Similarly, the National Geologic Mapping Act of 1992 grants USGS authority in

> (1) determining the Nation's geologic framework through systematic development of geologic maps at scales appropriate to the geologic setting and the perceived applications, such maps to be contributed to the national geologic map database; (2) development of a complementary national geophysical-map database, geochemical-map database, and a geochronologic and paleontologic database that provide value-added descriptive and interpretive information to the geologic-map database; (3) application of cost-effective mapping techniques that assemble, produce, translate and disseminate geologic-map information and that render such information of greater application and benefit to the public; and (4) development of public awareness for the role and application of geologic-map information to the resolution of national issues of land use management.[7]

Other relevant authorities granted to DOI include

- the establishment and location of permanent benchmarks used in the making of topographic surveys[8]
- publication of geological and economic maps, illustrating the resources and classification of the lands and reports upon general and economic geology and paleontology[9]
- surveying public lands[10]
- maintaining an archive of land remote sensing data for historical, scientific, and technical purposes, including long-term global environmental monitoring[11]

The Secretary of the Interior also has been designated certain responsibilities under the 2020 National Space Policy, which directs the Secretary, through USGS to

- conduct integrated predictive science, on natural and human-induced changes to Earth's land, land cover, and inland surface waters, and manage a national global land surface data archive and its distribution
- determine the operational requirements for collecting, processing, archiving, and distributing land surface data to the U.S. government

7 43 USC §31(a–h).
8 43 USC § 38.
9 43 USC § 41.
10 43 USC § 751.
11 51 USC § 60142.

- use international and commercial partnerships to help sustain and enhance land surface observations from space
- utilize, consistent with national security classification guidelines and sharing agreements and in coordination with the Secretary of Defense and the Director of National Intelligence, remote sensing information related to the environment and to disasters that is acquired from national security space systems

Many of these responsibilities require the Department of Interior to work closely with other agencies. For example, the 2020 National Space Policy directs the Secretary of Interior to work with NASA to maintain a sustainable land-imaging program for operational land remote sensing observations that meets the needs of United States users and leverages government, commercial, and international capabilities. In addition, the Secretary is directed to work with both NOAA and NASA to

- collaborate, as practicable, on future satellite and ground system architectures to ensure that civil space acquisition processes and capabilities are not unnecessarily duplicated
- continue to develop civil applications and information tools based on data collected by Earth observation satellites[12]

Another authority given to the Department of Interior is the operation and staffing of the Civil Application Committee (CAC). This authority was originally given to Department of Interior by President Ford in 1975.[13] The CAC provides oversight and facilitation of the use by civil agencies of defense and intelligence community satellite remote sensing data and capabilities. Federal civil agencies are permitted to use these resources, within their statutory mission provided they follow applicable laws and regulations protecting personal rights, personal privacy, and civil liberties and are authorized to do so.[14]

NOAA

NOAA plays a significant role in geospatial management within the United States. NOAA was essentially established in 1970 under an Executive Order

12 National Space Policy of the United States of America. (2020, December 9). Retrieved January 12, 2024, from https://trumpwhitehouse.archives.gov/wp-content/uploads/2020/12/National-Space-Policy.pdf.

13 Opstal, D. W. (2018). Sunk Cost, Well Spent: Enhancing Interagency Remote Sensing with the Civil Applications Committee. Civil Applications Committee Fact Sheet 2022–3002 Version 1.2, March 202, Retrieved January 14, 2024, from https://pubs.U.S. governments.gov/fs/2022/3002/fs20223002.pdf.

14 Id.

issued by President Nixon.[15] This Executive Order transferred several roles and responsibilities associated with geospatial information management to the newly established NOAA, including authorities under the Coast and Geodetic Survey Act of 1947 (33 U.S.C. §883 et seq.) to provide (i) charts and related information for the safe navigation of marine and air commerce and (ii) basic data for engineering and scientific purposes and for other commercial and industrial needs.[16]

Specific authorized activities of NOAA include preparing the following:

- hydrographic and topographic surveys
- geodetic control surveys
- field surveys for aeronautical charts
- geomagnetic, seismological, gravity, and related geophysical measurements and investigations and observations for the determination of variation in latitude and longitude

These authorities are spread across a number of different offices within NOAA. For example, NOAA's National Ocean Service is responsible for the National Geodetic Survey.[17] Its mission is to define, maintain, and provide access to the National Spatial Reference System (NSRS) to provide a consistent coordinate system throughout the United States that defines latitude, longitude, height, scale, gravity, and orientation. Pursuant to Section 33 U.S.C. § 883e, NOAA is authorized to enter into cooperative agreements for geodetic surveys, with states, localities, and other federal agencies. This includes accepting geodetic observations obtained by other federal, state, and local organizations to provide quality assurance, archiving, and distribution.[18] In furtherance of those objectives, the Department of Commerce has created model sharing agreements.[19]

The 2020 National Space Policy directs NOAA to take an active role in Earth observation. For example, NOAA is "responsible for the requirements, funding, and operation of civil environmental satellites and data-gathering in support of atmospheric and space weather forecasting." In another example of the need of interagency coordination, NASA also acts as the acquisition

15 White House, Reorganization Plan No. 4 (1970, July 9). Retrieved January 21, 2024, from https://darrp.noaa.gov/sites/default/files/Reorganization%20Plan%20No.%204%20of%20 1970.pdf.

16 As discussed in the next section, NOAA's authority includes granting licenses to operate commercial remote sensing satellites.

17 Coast and Geodetic Survey Act of 1947, 33 U.S.C. 883a et seq.

18 National Ocean Service. (n.d.). Policy Regarding the Incorporation of Geodetic Data of Other Organizations into the National Geodetic Survey Integrated Data Base.

19 See e.g., Department of Commerce Revised 883e Model Agreement Non-Federal, Retrieved January 21, 2024, from https://2010-2014.commerce.gov/sites/default/files/documents/2012/may/revised_883e_model_agreement_non-federal.pdf.

agent for NOAA's operational environmental satellites for those activities and programs, a role that has historically included the development, integration, testing, and launch of the nation's weather satellites.[20]

NASA

NASA also plays a significant role in federal geospatial information management. As NASA's primary mission is related to science, research and applications, its role in geospatial information management pertains to such matters as climate, disaster response, and agriculture. For example, NASA collects imagery and other types of data of weather systems to help forecasters predict the path of tropical storms, as well as understand large-scale environmental changes such as in ice cover, to advance climate science.

NASA's primary authority for geospatial information management comes from Section 51 USC § 20111 which grants NASA the authority to conduct several Earth observation activities. These activities include:

- planning, directing, and conducting aeronautical and space activities
- arranging for participation by the scientific community in planning scientific measurements and observations to be made through use of aeronautical and space vehicles and conducting (or arranging for the conduct) of such measurements and observations
- providing for the widest practicable and appropriate dissemination of information concerning its activities and associated results[21]

NASA uses those authorities to launch and operate a number of Earth observation satellites for scientific purposes. In addition, the agency operates in situ and aerial platforms that collect scientific data.[22]

In addition, the 2020 National Space Policy directs NASA's administrator, in coordination with the heads of other appropriate agencies, to

- conduct a program of research to understand Earth's interconnected systems, including the development of new Earth observation for other agencies to use for operational purposes
- develop a plan to provide Earth environmental satellite observation capabilities, including ground systems for operations, that meet current and future civil and national security requirements
- ensure the continued sharing of data from its systems

20 White House, National Space Policy of the United States of America. (2020, December 9).
21 51 U.S. Code § 20112.
22 NASA, Airborne Science Program. Retrieved January 14, 2024, from https://airbornescience.nasa.gov/aircraf.

Furthermore, it directs the NASA administrator to coordinate with other agencies, to (i) collaborate with academia, the commercial sector, and international partners to ensure uninterrupted operational environmental satellite observation; (ii) coordinate, on future satellite and ground system architectures to reduce duplication of space acquisition processes and capabilities; (iii) utilize international partnerships to sustain and enhance a robust Earth observations program that meets civil and national security requirements; and (iv) purchase commercial environmental data for use in meteorological and space weather models when appropriate.[23] While beyond the scope of this chapter, the reader should keep in mind that in providing direction and funding to NASA – as well as other agencies – Congress regularly impacts the execution of such responsibilities.

U.S. Group on Earth Observation (USGEO)

As noted previously, geospatial information management with the U.S. government requires significant coordination among government agencies. One example of such coordination is USGEO, a subcommittee under the White House National Science and Technology Council's Committee on the Environment, Natural Resources and Sustainability. It was established pursuant to the NASA Authorization Act of 2010[1] and is an interagency coordination mechanism for the various federal civil Earth observations activities across the U.S. government.

USGEO is chaired by the Office of Science and Technology Policy (OSTP). Its vice chairs are from NASA, NOAA, and USGS. Membership consists of both federal agencies and components of the White House. Its duties include

- coordinating, planning, and assessing federal Earth observation activities in cooperation with domestic stakeholders; and
- engaging interagency and national stakeholders to formulate the U.S. position for and coordinate U.S. participation in the international Group on Earth Observations (GEO)[24]

Through the Satellite Needs Working Group (SNWG), USGEO works with federal agencies to identify the U.S. government's future satellite Earth observations requirements. To meet this objective, the SNWG conducts a biennial survey, the results of which it communicates to NASA and other relevant agencies.[25] U.S. GEO also helps formulate and update the National Civil Plan

23 White House, National Space Policy of the United States of America. (2020, December 9).
24 U.S. Group on Earth Observations, Retrieved January 14, 2024, from https://usgeo.gov/.
25 U.S. Group on Earth Observations., Retrieved January 14, 2024, from https://usgeo.gov/working-groups.html.

for Earth Observations, a public document that seeks to "inform Federal investments in civil Earth observation systems."[26]

Conclusion

A number of civil federal agencies are responsible for managing different aspects of geospatial information. Their respective roles and responsibilities are set forth in a number of laws and policies, including the Geospatial Data Act of 2018, department and agency enabling legislation, in addition to various regulations and policies. As a result, geospatial information management within the U.S. can be a challenge as it requires significant coordination on matters such as budgeting, standards, data collection, maintenance, and sharing.

26 See e.g., U.S. Group On Earth Observations, Retrieved January 28, 2024 from https://usgeo.gov/national-plan.html.

11 Role of Defense and Intelligence Agencies in Geospatial Information Management

Geospatial Intelligence

Introduction

As is the case in most countries, the defense and intelligence agencies in the U.S. play a critical role in geospatial information management. This should not be surprising when one considers that the genesis of many geospatial technologies (e.g., surveying, satellite Earth observation, GPS, drones) are rooted in defense/intelligence applications.

Unfortunately, geospatial information management within the defense and intelligence agencies of the U.S. government is equally as complex as within civilian agencies. As with civil geospatial information management, there are a myriad of departments and agencies that have significant roles that are authorized by laws or regulations or granted by policies. For example, in addition to the National Geospatial-Intelligence Agency (NGA) and the National Reconnaissance Office (NRO), numerous other offices within the Department of Defense have responsibilities in the planning, procurement, and use of geospatial technologies and information. While some of these roles are more significant than others, major decisions often require coordination among numerous stakeholders with different missions and interests. There are also numerous laws, regulations, and policies that impact geospatial information management within the defense and intelligence communities. Understanding the legal and policy framework for geospatial information within the defense and intelligence communities becomes even more complicated because some of the policies and procedures are classified or otherwise restricted.[1]

Titles 10 and 50

In order to understand the legal and policy frameworks under which the defense and intelligence communities operate, it is important to begin with Title 10 and Title 50 of the United States Code. Each has a part in addressing

1 This chapter is based entirely upon materials that are publicly available.

DOI: 10.4324/9781003329961-11

the complicated roles that defense and intelligence agencies play (i.e., protecting the country from threats, while not using its resources to threaten the lives of citizens) in geospatial information management.

Title 10 sets the legal basis for the roles, missions, and organization of the Department of Defense and each of the armed services. Under Title 10, the U.S. military is given the authority to engage in traditional military activities, such as waging war, managing military installations, recruiting, and training military personnel, and procuring military equipment. Not surprisingly, geospatial technology plays important roles in a number of military applications.

Title 50, on the other hand, provides the legal foundation for most of the U.S. intelligence community's activities. This includes the Central Intelligence Agency (CIA), the National Security Agency (NSA), as well as other agencies when involved in intelligence or counterintelligence work. This authority, however, is subject to oversight and restrictions, particularly with regard to activities involving U.S. persons. In addition, given the nature of geospatial technology and information, it should not be a surprise that several agencies involved in geospatial information management operate under the authority of both Title 10 and Title 50.

To make matters even more complicated, the defense and intelligence agencies often use a different term for geospatial information management. It is often referred to as "geospatial intelligence" or "GEOINT." GEOINT is defined as the exploitation and analysis of imagery and geospatial information to describe, assess, and visually depict physical features and geographically referenced activities on or about Earth.[2] It consists of imagery, imagery intelligence, and other types of geospatial information.

National Geospatial Intelligence Agency (NGA)

NGA has had a long history with GEOINT. The agency was created on October 1, 1996, as the National Imagery and Mapping Agency (NIMA) by consolidating a number of defense and intelligence offices associated with geospatial intelligence. In 2003 it became the National Geospatial Intelligence Agency.[3]

NGA is subject to numerous legal and policy authorities pertaining to GEOINT. For purposes of geospatial law, three of the most important are (i) Title 10[4], (ii) Title 50,[5] and (iii) Executive Order 12333 (EO 12333). Collectively they detail an extensive list of roles and responsibilities for NGA in keeping with its role for GEOINT in the U.S.

2 10 USC 467(5).
3 PUBLIC LAW 108–136–NOV. 24, 2003, NATIONAL DEFENSE AUTHORIZATION ACT FOR FISCAL YEAR 2004.
4 10 USC Armed Forces.
5 50 USC War and National Defense.

Title 10 provides that one of NGA's primary missions is to support the combat mission of the Department of Defense.[6] In addition to supporting the combat commands, NGA's Title 10 responsibilities include (i) preparing and publishing maps, charts, and nautical books required for navigation (as directed by the Secretary of Defense)[7] and (ii) providing foreign countries, regional organizations with defense or security components and security alliances of which the U.S. is a member with imagery intelligence and geospatial information support.[8]

In addition, under Title 50, NGA is a member of the intelligence community.[9] As a result, on top of its Title 10 duties, NGA supports the geospatial intelligence requirements of departments and agencies of the United States.[10] Its Title 50 responsibilities include

- carrying out tasking of imagery collection
- coordinating imagery processing and exploitation activities
- ensuring the dissemination of imagery in a timely manner to authorized recipients
- prescribing technical architecture and standards related to imagery intelligence and geospatial information and ensuring compliance with such architecture and standards
- developing and fielding systems of common concern related to imagery intelligence and geospatial information[11]

Executive Order 12333 further outlines the responsibilities of the Director of NGA with respect to its responsibilities to assist the mission of the intelligence community.[12] These duties include

- providing geospatial intelligence support for national and departmental requirements and for the conduct of military operations
- conducting administrative and technical support activities within and outside the United States as necessary for covert arrangements
- collecting, processing, analyzing, producing, and disseminating geospatial intelligence information and data for foreign intelligence and counterintelligence purposes to support national and departmental missions
- conducting foreign geospatial intelligence liaison relationships

6 10 USC 441.
7 10 USC 451.
8 10 USC 454.
9 50 USC 3003.
10 50 USC 3045.
11 50 USC 3038(b).
12 The White House. (1981). Executive Order 12333 United States Intelligence Activities (As amended by Executive Orders 13284 (2003), 13355 (2004) and 13470 (2008)).

As a result of these separate legal authorities, the Director of NGA reports to both the Secretary of Defense as well as the Director of National Intelligence (DNI). This results in the NGA Director having to comply with a number of policies and directives.

For example, Department of Defense Directive Number 5105.60 (July 29, 2009) ("Directive 5105.60") describes many high-level responsibilities of the Director of NGA within the DoD hierarchy. These duties include

- acting as the principal advisor on GEOINT to the Secretary of Defense
- conducting all GEOINT activities delegated under the authorities of the Secretary of Defense as the DoD GEOINT manager
- Serving as the GEOINT functional manager
- planning, organizing, directing, and managing NGA and all assigned resources, to provide peacetime, contingency, crisis, and combat GEOINT support to the operational military forces of the United States

Directive Number 5105.60 further describes NGA's specific roles and responsibilities. A detailed list of the roles and responsibilities is beyond the scope of this book, but a number pertain to GEOINT, such as

- providing responsive GEOINT products, support, services, and information
- planning and prioritization of validated collection requirements
- managing GEOINT planning, collection, operations, analysis, production, and dissemination
- establishing and/or consolidating DoD geospatial information collection requirements
- reviewing and responding to GEOINT requirements and priorities for military operations in support of the chairman of the Joint Chiefs of Staff and the Combatant Commanders
- identifying and analyzing the industrial base, as appropriate, to meet essential national GEOINT requirements
- participating in Secretary of Defense and DNI acquisition processes

DoD Instruction Number 3115.5 December 6, 2011, Incorporating Change 2, October 1, 2020 (Instruction Number 3115.5) further defines NGA's role and responsibilities. For example, it designates NGA as the DoD lead for GEOINT standards. Its duties include prescribing, mandating, and enforcing standards and architectures related to GEOINT and GEOINT tasking, collection, processing, and exploitation. NGA also represents the Department of Defense in national and international geospatial information standard organizations standards and architectures related to GEOINT for the DoD Components and for the non-DoD elements of the Intelligence Community.

Functional Manager of GEOINT

With respect to its responsibilities to the DNI, the director of NGA serves as functional manager for GEOINT.[13] These duties include (i) developing and implementing strategic guidance, policies, and procedures for activities; (ii) setting training and tradecraft standards; and (iii) ensuring coordination within and across intelligence disciplines and Intelligence Community elements.[14]

National Reconnaissance Office (NRO)

The National Reconnaissance Office (NRO) also has a significant role in GEOINT due to its role in satellite reconnaissance, including Earth observation. Also like NGA, from a GEOINT perspective it has legal authorities under Title 10, Title 50, and Executive Order 12333. As a result, the director of the NRO too has responsibilities to both the Secretary of Defense and the DNI.

The NRO is responsible for research and development, acquisition, launch, deployment, and operation of overhead reconnaissance systems, to support U.S. government needs. Also, under the authority, direction, and control of the undersecretary of defense for intelligence, the director of the NRO serves as the principal advisor on overhead reconnaissance to the Secretary of Defense, the Chairman of the Joint Chiefs of Staff, the Combatant Commanders, the Secretary of the Air Force, and the DoD Executive Agent (EA) for Space.[15]

As the principal advisor for overhead reconnaissance, the director of the NRO is responsible for

- providing the principal interface between overhead reconnaissance and other military domains
- recommending proposed overhead reconnaissance space architectures
- leading and managing NRO commercial partnerships, and industrial and supplier base issues that involve overhead reconnaissance
- ensuring NRO activities are integrated, when appropriate, within the DoD and with programs of the National Aeronautics and Space Administration
- maintaining partnerships across organizational boundaries with other members of the Intelligence Community[16]

13 The White House. (1981). Executive Order 12333 United States Intelligence Activities (As amended by Executive Orders 13284 (2003), 13355 (2004) and 13470 (2008)).

14 Director of National Intelligence. (2009, May). *Intelligence community directive number 113 (Functional Managers)*. Retrieved January 15, 2024, from www.odni.gov/files/documents/ICD/ICD_113.pdf.

15 U.S. Department of Defense. (2011). DoDD 5105.23, National Reconnaissance Office (NRO).

16 U.S. Department of Defense. (2011). DoDD 5105.23, National Reconnaissance Office (NRO).

Executive Order 12333 also sets forth duties for NRO. These duties include (i) preparing a comprehensive NRO program and budget input, and (ii) planning and conducting overhead reconnaissance research and development. In addition, as noted in Chapter 9, the Trump Administration shifted the authority to purchase commercial satellite imagery from NGA to the NRO.

Other GEOINT Roles Within the Department of Defense

While NGA and the NRO have significant roles and responsibilities within the DoD regarding GEOINT, several laws and policies give other offices within DoD important roles as well. As is the case within civil geospatial information management, this structure adds to the complexity of GEOINT. For example, within the Department of Defense alone

- the Heads of the DoD Components are responsible for (i) consulting with the director of NGA on requirements definition (and subsequent phases) for systems requiring unique GEOINT data, products, or services and (ii) coordinating with the Director of NGA when proposing or overseeing new GEOINT-related activities or programs
- the Director of the Defense Intelligence Agency is responsible for coordinating with the Combatant Commands to synchronize DoD intelligence, surveillance, and reconnaissance resources with other collection activities, and monitor execution of GEOINT collection operations
- the chairman of the Joint Chiefs of Staff, monitors, reports findings, and makes recommendations to the Secretary of Defense regarding the responsiveness of the NGA to military requirements and responds to Combatant Commander requests for military GEOINT systems, units, or other assets and coordinate the allocation of resources accordingly[17]

More recently, the United States Space Force, created pursuant to 10 U.S. Code § 9081, has begun to play a larger role in geospatial information management. For example, in addition to its role in the procurement of commercial satellite imagery,[18] a Commercial Augmented Space Reserve, under consideration within the U.S. government, would be under the authority of the Space Force.[19]

17 Department of Defense. (2020, October 1). *DoD Instruction Number 3115.5 December 6, 2011, Incorporating Change 2, October 1, 2020.* Retrieved January 14, 2024, from www.esd.whs.mil/Portals/54/Documents/DD/issuances/dodi/311515p.PDF?ver=soXmrmCmP4hJi-LhFahaeg%3D%3D.

18 See Chapter 9 for a discussion of the role of the Space Force in acquiring commercial satellite imagery.

19 Erwin, S. (2023, July 25). *Space News Space Force to further define details of a 'commercial space reserve.* Retrieved January 12, 2024, from https://spacenews.com/space-force-to-further-define-details-of-a-commercial-space-reserve/.

Director of National Intelligence

The legal framework in the U.S. also gives several other departments outside of the DoD responsibilities for GEOINT. As noted earlier in the chapter, the DNI oversees the entire Intelligence Community, which includes 18 individual agencies and organizations, one of which is NGA.[20] As a result, it has a significant role in many operational aspects of GEOINT.

Department of Homeland Security

The Department of Homeland Security was established in 2002 – combining 22 different federal departments and agencies into a unified, integrated Cabinet agency – pursuant to the Homeland Security Act of 2002.[21] In carrying out the responsibilities assigned in the Homeland Security Act of 2002, as amended, the Secretary of Homeland Security

- evaluates national capabilities, opportunities, and challenges in protecting critical infrastructure
- analyzes threats to and vulnerabilities of critical infrastructure
- identifies security and resilience functions that are necessary for effective public-private engagement with all critical infrastructure sectors
- develops a national plan and metrics, in coordination with critical infrastructure partners
- integrates and coordinates federal security and resilience activities
- reports on the effectiveness of national efforts to strengthen the nation's security and resilience posture for critical infrastructure

Similarly, President Policy Directive 21 states that the secretary of Homeland Security shall provide strategic guidance, promote a national unity of effort, and coordinate the overall federal effort to promote the security and resilience of the nation's critical infrastructure.

Given the nexus of geospatial information and critical infrastructure, DHS has several important duties associated with GEOINT. For example, the HIFLD subcommittee discussed in Chapter 6 is operated by DHS. The DHS Geospatial Management Office (GMO) was created to exercise "executive leadership" in establishing the department's geospatial information and technology programs and ensuring the security of geospatial information, software, hardware, and applications.[22] The office also serves as the DHS

20 50 U.S. Code § 3024–Responsibilities and authorities of the Director of National Intelligence.

21 Public Law 107–2961 116 Stat. 21352.

22 Department of Homeland Security. (2004, November 12). *Geospatial Management Office, Department of Homeland Security Management Directive System MD Number: 4030.* Retrieved January 21, 2024, from www.dhs.gov/xlibrary/assets/foia/mgmt_directive_4030_geospatial_management_office.pdf.

representative to federal geospatial executive steering committees, including the FGDC Steering Committee.[23]

Positioning, Navigation, and Timing (PNT)

Another aspect of geospatial information management that requires coordination among various elements of the U.S. government is PNT. PNT is also subject to a variety of laws in the United States. For example, both Title 10 and Title 51 (National and Commercial Space Programs) address matters associated with GPS. Title 10 authorizes the Secretary of Defense to operate and sustain GPS for both military and civil purposes free of direct user fees.[24] The Secretary of Defense is directed to coordinate with the Secretary of Transportation on GPS requirements and augmentation and with the Secretary of Commerce (and others) to facilitate civil and commercial uses as well as to implement measures to prevent hostile use of GPS. The Council on Oversight of the Department of Defense Positioning, Navigation, and Timing Enterprise is responsible for oversight of the Department of Defense positioning, navigation, and timing enterprise, including services provided to civil, commercial, scientific, and international users.[25]

Similarly, Title 51 encourages the continuous, worldwide operation of GPS free of direct user fees. It also encourages the president to

> provide clear direction and adequate resources to the Assistant Secretary of Commerce for Communications and Information so that on an international basis the Assistant Secretary can (i) achieve and sustain efficient management of the electromagnetic spectrum used by the Global Positioning System; and (ii) protect that spectrum from disruption and interference.[26]

President Trump issued Space Policy Directive 7 (SPD-7) in 2021 to replace the National Security Presidential Directive-39 (NSPD-39) issued on December 15, 2004. The stated goal of SPD-7 was to maintain United States leadership in global navigation satellite systems. SPD-7 directs the United States government to

- provide continuous worldwide access to U.S. space-based GPS services and government-provided augmentations, free of direct user fees
- operate and maintain GPS in accordance with U.S. law to satisfy civil, homeland security, and national security needs

23 *Id.*
24 Title 10 United States Code, Section 2281.
25 Title 10 of the U.S. Code, Section 2279b.
26 51 U.S.C. §50112.

- improve capabilities to deny hostile use of U.S. government space-based PNT services, without unduly disrupting civil and commercial access to civil PNT services
- improve the performance of U.S. space-based PNT services
- improve the cybersecurity of GPS and foster private sector adoption of cyber-secure GPS enabled system
- protect GPS spectrum and work with U.S. industry to investigate additional areas of the radio spectrum which could increase GPS and PNT resilience

SPD-7 also created a joint civil/military body for guiding and preserving the federal government interests in the provision of space-based PNT services, augmentations, and space-based alternatives. The responsibilities of the National Executive Committee for Space-Based Positioning, Navigation include[27]

- ensuring that national security, homeland security, and civil requirements receive full and appropriate consideration in the decision-making process
- coordinating space-based PNT program plans, requirements, budget considerations and policies
- promoting, reviewing, and implementing plans to modernize United States space-based PNT infrastructure and services
- coordinating with the Office of Science and Technology Policy to promote research and development on next-generation technologies

Conclusion

The defense and intelligence communities play an important role in geospatial information management within the U.S. As is the case with civil geospatial information management, multiple defense and intelligence agencies have a role. This requires significant coordination among and within agencies. In addition, there are several key issues that require coordination between civil and defense/intelligence aspects of the geospatial ecosystem.

27 Other members include Department of State, Department of the Treasury, Department of Justice, Department of the Interior, Department of Agriculture, Department of Commerce, Department of Energy, Department of Homeland Security, Office of the Director of National Intelligence, Joint Chiefs of Staff, National Aeronautics and Space Administration, and National Telecommunications and Information Administration (ex-officio).

12 Where Geospatial Technology Is Taking the Law

Introduction

The law in the U.S. tends to trail technological developments. That is why although adoption of geospatial technology and applications using geospatial information have increased, the legal and regulatory community has not kept pace. However, as this book has tried to highlight, that is beginning to change. Existing laws are being applied – or interpreted to apply – to geospatial information management. Alternatively, new laws and regulations are being introduced. In addition, the courts are being asked to address cases with significant geospatial implications. All of these will likely have a significant impact on the collection, use, analysis, distribution, and storage of geospatial information.

There are two additional trends to watch with respect to geospatial law. The first is the use of geospatial technology and information to address transnational issues. Geospatial technology could play a significant role in addressing issues such as climate change and food security. However, this will require sharing of geospatial information across borders, which raises significant legal issues.

In addition, new technologies – such as AI, autonomous vehicles, and the Internet of Things – are causing lawmakers and regulators to develop new laws and regulations. Although these technologies are not necessarily considered geospatial, they are often related to the geospatial ecosystem, either as collectors or consumers of geospatial information. As a result, any new laws and regulations will surely impact geospatial technologies.

Transnational Issues

There has been a significant increase in the adoption of geospatial technologies and applications that use geospatial information. This has resulted in an increased understanding of the potential for geospatial technologies to address significant global issues. In combatting climate change, satellites can be used to measure and track the levels of carbon dioxide and other greenhouse gases in the atmosphere. This information can help policy makers

DOI: 10.4324/9781003329961-12

better understand the sources and levels of emissions and how they can be reduced. Similarly, geospatial information can be used to monitor ocean temperature, sea level rise, and ocean acidification, which are all key indicators of the impacts of climate change. Geospatial information also plays critical roles in monitoring deforestation and in climate models, which can be used to predict the effects of climate change on Earth's systems and help inform policy decisions.

Geospatial technology can also be used to monitor human rights violations. For example, geospatial information can assist in (i) tracking forced displacement, (ii) monitoring conflict zones, (iii) detecting mass graves, (iv) identifying destroyed infrastructure, (v) assessing environmental damage, and (vi) verifying reports and testimonies. This information can then serve as evidence in legal proceedings or support advocacy campaigns to raise awareness and pressure governments to address human rights abuses.

Issues Limiting the Sharing of Geospatial Information to Address Critical Transnational Issues

This textbook has highlighted some of the legal and ethical challenges associated with geospatial information management within a country. These challenges become much more complex when geospatial information is being shared with stakeholders outside of a country, which is almost inevitable when dealing with transnational issues. For example, the licensing issues become more complex when aggregating geospatial information from different countries. One of the primary reasons is that the laws of each jurisdiction are very different on matters such as privacy/data protection, intellectual property rights, and liability. For instance, government agencies in some countries charge users a fee to use their geospatial information to cover their costs (or increase their budget). They are concerned about broadly sharing this information or licensing it under an open data license.

Similarly, the national security concerns associated with geospatial information vary between countries. Some countries have restrictions on what types of information can be shared. For example, China announced restrictions on the sharing of certain types of geospatial information due to national security concerns.[1]

Use of Geospatial Information for Compliance

Geospatial information can play an important role in transnational issues through monitoring compliance with laws, regulations, voluntary targets, and even norms. Several organizations use geospatial information to monitor

1 Brar, A. (2023, December 14). China locks down GPS data to guard state secrets. *Newsweek*. Retrieved from www.newsweek.com/china-gps-data-spies-technology-state-secret-investigation-1852398

compliance with environmentally friendly standards and practices. For example, the Roundtable on Sustainable Palm Oil (RSPO) uses geospatial information to monitor compliance with its standards for sustainable palm oil production.[2]

However, the real value for geospatial information in this context will be when it can be used at the international level in courts of law or otherwise in enforcement. International courts have been asked to consider satellite remote sensing imagery and other types of geospatial information on several occasions.[3] However, there are numerous challenges in using this information as evidence, particularly in international tribunals.[4] Many of these have to do with the challenges associated with using any new technology in a court proceeding. As Quilling notes in a recent paper on the subject:

> In the digital age, new technologies and advancements in computing power have transformed how potentially relevant evidence of atrocities will be evaluated in international criminal law. New technologies make possible the aggregation of data related to armed conflict from a rich array of sources including, but not limited to, satellite and geospatial imagery, Global Positioning Systems (GPS), mobile phone data, videos, photographs, social media, and other Internet sources (Koenig et al., 2021, pp. 14–21). The International Criminal Court (ICC or "the Court") is presently underprepared for the increasingly central challenges of authenticating digital evidence and has struggled to adapt to these changes.[5]

Similarly, a report from the Asser Institute states that

> images acquired by satellites have become key sources of information and evidence within the international criminal justice system. Yet, their use remains hampered by the lack of technological proficiency among legal professionals on one hand and by the unfamiliarity with the legal field among satellite imagery experts on the other.[6]

2 RSPO. (n.d.). *How GIS technology helps keep RSPO members accountable*. Retrieved January 9, 2024, from https://rspo.org/how-gis-technology-helps-keep-rspo-members-accountable/.

3 Chaturvedi, S. (2015, January 8). Satellite imagery in international human rights litigation. *American Association for the Advancement of Science*. Retrieved January 12, 2024, from www.aaas.org/news/satellite-imagery-international-human-rights-litigation.

4 See e.g., Macauley, E. D. (n.d.). The role satellites (should) play in the protection and promotion of human rights, including the use of Earth observation satellites in evidential matters. *International Criminal Court (ICC)*. Retrieved January 12, 2024, from www.mcgill.ca/iasl/files/iasl/wef-mcgill_space-macauley.pdf.

5 Quilling, C. (2022, May 20). The future of digital evidence authentication at the International Criminal Court. *Princeton Journal of Public and International Affairs*. Retrieved January 9, 2024, from https://jpia.princeton.edu/news/future-digital-evidence-authentication-international-criminal-court.

6 Asser Institute. (n.d.). *Satellite imagery as evidence in international justice proceedings*. Retrieved January 9, 2024, from www.asser.nl/projects-legal-advice/projects/?rId=1174.

There are two important considerations from a geospatial law standpoint. First, the use of geospatial information in a court case requires that the information be shared across jurisdictions. This results in several of the same issues as those associated with licensing.

There are two primary ways to share evidence. The Evidence Convention, formally known as the Convention on the Taking of Evidence Abroad in Civil or Commercial Matters, is an international treaty that aims to facilitate the taking of evidence across national borders in civil or commercial matters.[7] The purpose of the Evidence Convention is to provide a framework for the recognition and enforcement of requests for evidence in civil or commercial cases that involve parties or evidence located in different countries.

Mutual Legal Assistance Agreements (MLA) are formal agreements between two or more countries to facilitate and improve cooperation in investigating and prosecuting criminal offenses.[8] The purpose of an MLA is to provide a legal framework for sharing information and evidence between countries in order to assist in the investigation and prosecution of criminal offenses that cross national borders.

The second issue involves authentication of the geospatial information to be used in a court proceeding. Courts generally do not allow a piece of evidence to be used without being authenticated for its accuracy and provenance. For example, the procedures for authenticating aerial photographs in a court case may vary depending on the jurisdiction and the specific circumstances of the case, but generally the process requires showing that it is a true and accurate representation of what the image purports to depict. This often is done through testimony from an expert witness who can vouch for the authenticity of the photograph.

The opposing party may object to the admissibility of the geospatial information based on lack of foundation, authentication, or other grounds. The court will consider these objections and rule on whether the geospatial information may be admitted into evidence. Even if the geospatial information is admitted into evidence, the court may consider its weight or probative value in deciding the case. This will depend on factors such as the credibility of the witness who authenticated the geospatial information, its quality, and its relevance to the issues in the case.

In the U.S. there are two primary standards to determine the admissibility of expert testimony based on new technologies: the Frye Rule and the Daubert Rule. The main difference lies in their approach to determining the reliability of

7 Hague Conference on Private International Law. (n.d.). *Convention on the taking of evidence abroad in civil or commercial matters*. Retrieved January 9, 2024, from https://assets.hcch.net/docs/dfed98c0-6749-42d2-a9be-3d41597734f1.pdf.

8 See e.g., U.S. Department of Justice, Office of International Affairs. (n.d.). *Mutual legal assistance treaties of the United States*. Retrieved January 9, 2024, from www.justice.gov/criminal-oia/file/1498806/download#:~:text=Treaties%20on%20Mutual%20Legal%20Assistance,courts%20of%20the%20Requesting%20State.

the scientific evidence presented. The Frye Rule emphasizes the general acceptance of scientific techniques in the field. On the other hand, the Daubert Rule emphasizes the reliability and relevance of the scientific evidence presented.

The issue of reliability of geospatial information arose in the case *Ohio v. Franklin.*[9] The issue in the case was whether the defendant had sold drugs within 1,000 feet of a schoolyard. The defendant challenged a police officer's use of GIS software to measure the distance between the sale and the school. The defendant argued that the technology was scientific and that the testimony given by a city GIS testimony was not sufficient to admit it as evidence. The prosecutor argued the technology was widely used and generally reliable. The judge, in denying the defendant's challenge, stated, "[W]hether the GIS employed by Det. Bucheit was used properly and measured the distance accurately goes to the weight, not the sufficiency, of the evidence presented."

New Technologies Raising New Concerns

Another driving force for geospatial law is the rollout of new technologies that collect and/or use geospatial information. For example, autonomous vehicles are raising questions about liability issues.[10] As discussed in an earlier chapter, drones raise questions about privacy and national security. Surprisingly, even balloons have made a comeback, raising national security issues.[11] Also, there is a class action case against Apple concerning the tracking capabilities of air tags.[12] All of these indicate that lawmakers and regulators are paying closer attention to the risks associated with geospatial information. For example, the Health and Location Data Protection Act would ban data brokers from selling health and location data.[13] At the local level, New York City's Tenant Data Privacy Law protects information collected from buildings with "smart access" technology, including location data.[14]

9 164 Ohio App 3d 758 (12th Dist. 2005).

10 The Verge. (2023, October 31). *Tesla wins another court case by arguing fatal Autopilot crash was caused by human error*. Retrieved January 11, 2024, from www.theverge.com/2023/10/31/23940693/tesla-jury-autopilot-win-liable-micah-lee.

11 NBC News. (2023, April 3). *Chinese spy balloon gathered intelligence from sensitive U.S. military sites, despite U.S. Efforts to block it*. Retrieved January 11, 2024, from www.nbcnews.com/politics/national-security/china-spy-balloon-collected-intelligence-us-military-bases-rcna77155.

12 The Register. (2023, October 13). *Three dozen plaintiffs join Apple AirTag tracking lawsuit in amended complaint*. Retrieved January 11, 2024, from www.theregister.com/2023/10/13/three_dozen_plaintiffs_join_apple_airtag_suit/ accessed January 11, 2024.

13 See e.g., Warren, E. (n.d.). *Health and location data protection Act*. Retrieved January 11, 2024, from www.warren.senate.gov/imo/media/doc/Health%20and%20Location%20Data%20Protection%20Act.pdf.

14 See e.g., New York City Council. (n.d.). *Tenant data privacy law*. Retrieved January 11, 2024, from https://legistar.council.nyc.gov/LegislationDetail.aspx?ID=4196254&GUID=29A4B0E2-4C1F-472B-AE88-AE10B5313AC1&Options=ID%7cText%7c&Search=.

Artificial Intelligence

AI is likely to be the technology with the biggest impact from a geospatial law standpoint. One of the primary reasons is that due to the technology's vast potential, lawmakers and regulators across the globe are scrambling to develop legal frameworks that balance the benefits of AI with its potential risk. Second, the legal concerns associated with AI are those similar to those have been addressed in this book: intellectual property rights, privacy, liability and data quality, national security, and licensing. Finally, the geospatial community has been using AI for a long time, so any new laws and regulations are more likely to impact those organizations than those that are just beginning to use this exciting new technology.

This textbook has explained the multiple roles the government plays in the geospatial community. The federal government also has multiple roles with respect to AI – as a consumer, as a regulator, and as a promoter of the technology. You can see some of this tension is the legal and regulatory framework that is developing in the U.S.

In October 2023, the White House issued an Executive Order on AI.[15] The Executive Order is a comprehensive effort to outline the role of the federal government in both protecting against the potential risks of AI and harnessing its tremendous potential. Key aspects of the Executive Order include the following:

Safety, Security, and Trustworthiness – The Executive Order mandates developing standards, tools, and tests to ensure AI systems are safe, secure, and trustworthy.

Privacy Protection – The Executive Order calls for the development and use of privacy-preserving techniques, including AI technologies that allow training AI systems while preserving data privacy.

Equity and Civil Rights – The Executive Order seeks to address and mitigate algorithmic discrimination and biases in various sectors, including labor and housing markets, by directing federal agencies to research these issues and develop guidelines and policies.

Consumer, Patient, and Student Protection – The Executive Order aims to harness AI's benefits for consumers, healthcare, and education, while safeguarding against potential harm. This includes establishing safety programs for AI in healthcare and developing resources for educators using AI-enabled tools.

National Security and International Engagement – The Executive Order includes provisions related to national security, directing efforts to counter

15 The White House. (2023, October 30). *Executive order on the safe, secure, and trustworthy development and use of artificial intelligence*. Retrieved January 21, 2024, from www.whitehouse.gov/briefing-room/presidential-actions/2023/10/30/executive-order-on-the-safe-secure-and-trustworthy-development-and-use-of-artificial-intelligence/.

adversaries' military use of AI and engaging with international allies on common AI governance frameworks.

Regulation and Industry Standards – The Executive Order emphasizes the need for fair competition and the protection of consumers and workers from AI-enabled harm. It also encourages the private sector to align its AI development and use with the policy positions of the Order.

Implementation and Compliance – Various federal agencies are tasked with implementing the Order's provisions, with specific deadlines and requirements for action. The Order also involves public input and feedback mechanisms to refine its implementation.

The Executive Order directs several government agencies to take an active role in implementation. For example, NIST is tasked with developing standards, tools, and tests to ensure the safety, security, and trustworthiness of AI systems, and the Department of Commerce is directed to establish detailed reporting requirements for companies developing certain types of AI models, particularly regarding dual-use foundation models and for developing guidance for content authentication and watermarking to label AI-generated content. Similarly, the Federal Trade Commission (FTC) is directed to use its rulemaking authority to ensure fair competition in the AI marketplace and to protect consumers and workers from AI-enabled harms, and the Office of Management and Budget (OMB) is directed to develop guidance for agencies on AI risk management, testing, and the mitigation of bias and discrimination in AI models.

In connection with the Executive Order, federal agencies took several steps that could have an impact on geospatial organizations. For example, the Consumer Financial Protect Bureau, the Equal Employment Opportunity Commission, and the FTC issued guidance regarding employment and other types of discrimination using AI,[16] and the Copyright Office solicited comments as to how copyright law should apply to AI systems.[17] The Department of Defense published its Responsible Artificial Intelligence (RAI) Toolkit, which incorporates its own AI Ethical Principles and NIST's AI Risk Management Framework into the development of AI products for DoD.[18]

16 Federal Trade Commission. *EEOC-CRT-FTC-CFPB-AI-Joint-Statement.* Retrieved January 12, 2024, from www.ftc.gov/system/files/ftc_gov/pdf/EEOC-CRT-FTC-CFPB-AI-Joint-Statement%28final%29.pdf.

17 Federal Register. (2023, August 30). *Artificial intelligence and copyright.* Retrieved January 12, 2024, from www.federalregister.gov/documents/2023/08/30/2023-18624/artificial-intelligence-and-copyright.

18 Department of Defense. (n.d.). *CDAO Releases Responsible AI (RAI) toolkit for ensuring alignment with RAI best practices.* Retrieved January 12, 2024, from www.defense.gov/News/Releases/Release/Article/3588743/cdao-releases-responsible-ai-rai-toolkit-for-ensuring-alignment-with-rai-best-p/.

Several bills have been introduced in Congress to regulate AI. For example, in November 2023, the Artificial Intelligence Research, Innovation, and Accountability Act of 2023 (AIRIA) was introduced. The AIRIA is a comprehensive, bipartisan bill that tries to encourage AI innovation while also establishing a framework for transparency and accountability.[19]

It would create two categories of AI systems: high-impact and critical-impact, each with different regulatory requirements. Critical-Impact AI System is defined as an artificial intelligence system that is

- deployed for a purpose other than solely for use by the Department of Defense or an intelligence agency and
- used or intended to be used
- to make decisions that have a legal or similarly significant effect on
    - (i) the real-time or ex post facto collection of biometric data of natural persons by biometric identification systems without their consent
    - (ii) the direct management and operation of critical infrastructure and space-based infrastructure or
    - (iii) criminal justice, and
- in a manner that poses a significant risk to rights afforded under the Constitution of the United States or safety

Organizations that deployed Critical-Impact AI Systems would be required to perform a risk management assessment. Assessments would be required to include

- policies, processes, procedures, and practices across the organization relating to transparent and effective mapping, measuring, and managing of artificial intelligence risks
- the structure, context, and capabilities of the critical-impact artificial intelligence system or critical-impact foundation model
- a description of how the organization employs quantitative, qualitative, or mixed-method tools, techniques, and methodologies to analyze, assess, benchmark, and monitor artificial intelligence risk
- a description of allocation of risk resources to map and measure risks on a regular basis.

However, organizations that deployed High-Impact Artificial Intelligence Systems would only have to adhere to transparency reporting obligations. A High-impact Artificial Intelligence System means an artificial intelligence

19 118th Congress. (2023–2024). *S.3312. 2024 artificial intelligence research, innovation, and accountability Act of 2023*. Retrieved January 12, 2024, from www.congress.gov/bill/118th-congress/senate-bill/3312/text?s=1&r=7.

system that is (i) deployed for a purpose other than solely for use by the Department of Defense or an intelligence agency and (ii) specifically developed with the intended purpose of making decisions that have a legal or similarly significant effect on the access of an individual to housing, employment, credit, education, health care, or insurance in a manner that poses a significant risk to safety or constitutionally afforded rights. Similar obligations are imposed on the developers of High-Impact and Critical Impact AI Systems.

In addition, AIRIA would expand what qualifies as open data to include data models, defined as "a mathematical, economic, or statistical representation of a system or process used to assist in making calculations and predictions, including through the use of algorithms, computer programs, or artificial intelligence systems."

Court cases involving AI could also have a significant impact on geospatial information management. For example, in December 2023, the New York Times filed a detailed lawsuit against OpenAI alleging that in using articles for training its ChatGPT, OpenAI violated NYT's copyright. OpenAI's defense is that its use is protected by the fair use doctrine.

The geospatial community has been using AI for a long time, so any new laws and regulations are more likely to impact those organizations than those that are just beginning to use it.

Regulation of AI is also occurring at the state level. For example, comprehensive data protection laws in states such as California and Virginia already address the use of AI for profiling. California also has a law that regulates AI to protect against employment discrimination. In addition, a number of states have passed executive orders concerning AI.

What Should Geospatial Professionals Do?

In anticipation of the proposed AI regulation and legislation requiring transparency and oversight of training data, models, and generated content, geospatial professionals should take several steps.

Firstly, understanding the data supply chain is crucial. This involves not just "data mapping" but a comprehensive understanding of how data is collected or obtained, used within the organization, and shared with third parties. Geospatial professionals should be aware of the type of data being used, how it was obtained (whether it was collected, produced, or acquired), and what legal protections or requirements apply, whether contractual or regulatory.

Secondly, it's important to know who within an organization has access to the data and how the data is used. This includes understanding what products and services are created using the data, whether it is aggregated with other types, and if such aggregation is allowed under applicable agreements. Additionally, professionals should be aware of how long the data is retained and what the contractual or regulatory requirements are for data storage.

Lastly, when it comes to sharing data with third parties, geospatial professionals should know in what form the data is shared. They should also be aware of the contractual or regulatory requirements that apply when sharing data and make sure applicable requirements are passed on to third parties.

Conclusion

The value of geospatial information from an economic, governmental, and societal standpoint is becoming broadly recognized. However, this textbook has highlighted the legal issues that impact geospatial information management within the U.S. These issues are particularly complex due in part to the versatility of geospatial information, particularly given the dual use of many geospatial applications, the diversity of the geospatial community and the need to aggregate different geospatial information datasets to create products and services. As geospatial becomes more mainstream, it will become increasingly important for geospatial professionals to proactively engage with the legal and policy communities to develop a framework that enables geospatial technology to achieve its full potential while adequately addressing significant risks. This book provides geospatial law professionals with the context to meaningly contribute to these discussions.

References

Asser Institute. (n.d.). *Satellite imagery as evidence in international justice proceedings*. Retrieved January 9, 2024, from www.asser.nl/projects-legal-advice/projects/?rId=1174.

Brar, A. (2023, December 14). China locks down GPS data to guard state secrets. *Newsweek*. Retrieved from www.newsweek.com/china-gps-data-spies-technology-state-secret-investigation-1852398.

Chaturvedi, S. (2015, January 8). Satellite imagery in international human rights litigation. *American Association for the Advancement of Science*. Retrieved January 12, 2024, from www.aaas.org/news/satellite-imagery-international-human-rights-litigation.

Koenig, Alexa, Emma Irving, Yvonne McDermott, and Daragh Murray. 2021. "New Technologies and the Investigation of International Crimes: An Introduction." *Journal of International Criminal Justice* 19 (1): 1–7

Macauley, E. D. (n.d.). The role satellites (should) play in the protection and promotion of human rights, including the use of earth observation satellites in evidential matters. *International Criminal Court (ICC)*. Retrieved January 12, 2024, from www.mcgill.ca/iasl/files/iasl/wef-mcgill_space-macauley.pdf.

NBC News. (2023, April 3). *Chinese spy balloon gathered intelligence from sensitive U.S. military sites, despite U.S. efforts to block it*. Retrieved January 11, 2024, from www.nbcnews.com/politics/national-security/china-spy-balloon-collected-intelligence-us-military-bases-rcna77155.

The Register. (2023, October 13). *Three dozen plaintiffs join Apple AirTag tracking lawsuit in amended complaint*. Retrieved January 11, 2024, from www.theregister.com/2023/10/13/three_dozen_plaintiffs_join_apple_airtag_suit/. Accessed January 11, 2024.

RSPO. (n.d.). *How GIS technology helps keep RSPO members accountable*. Retrieved January 9, 2024, from https://rspo.org/how-gis-technology-helps-keep-rspo-members-accountable/.

Quilling, C. (2022, May 20). The future of digital evidence authentication at the international criminal court. *Princeton Journal of Public and International Affairs*. Retrieved January 9, 2024, from https://jpia.princeton.edu/news/future-digital-evidence-authentication-international-criminal-court.

Warren, E. (n.d.). *Health and location data protection Act*. Retrieved January 11, 2024, from www.warren.senate.gov/imo/media/doc/Health%20and%20Location%20Data%20Protection%20Act.pdf.

Additional Readings

Aganaba-Jeanty, T. (2017, November). Satellites remote sensing and big data: Legal implications for measuring emissions. *CIGI Papers No. 151*. Center for International Governance Innovation.

Cho, G. (2008). *Geographic information service: Mastering the legal issues*. Wiley.

Compendium on the Licensing of Geospatial Information. (n.d.). United Nations Committee of Experts on Global Geospatial Information Management.

Congressional Research Service. (2009, June 8). *Geospatial information and geographic information systems (GIS): Current issues and future challenges*. Retrieved April 20, 2024, from https://sgp.fas.org/crs/misc/R40625.pdf.

Department of Defense. (2009, July 29). Directive Number 5105.60.

Department of Defense. (2011, June 28). Directive Number 5105.23.

Federal Geographic Data Committee, Homeland Security Working Group. (2005, June). *Guidelines for providing appropriate access to geospatial data in response to security concerns*. Retrieved April 20, 2024, from https://www.fgdc.gov/policyandplanning/Access%20Guidelines.pdf.

Glazer, R., Lebowitz, J., & Greenberg, M. (2013). *Data as IP and data license agreements*. Practical Law.

Ito, A. (2007). Improvement to the legal regime for the effective use of satellite remote sensing data for disaster management and protection of the environment. *Journal of Space Law*, *34*.

Janssen, K., & Compvoets, J. (2012). *Geographic data and the law: Defining new challenges*. Leuven University Press.

National Research Council. (2004). *Licensing geographic data and services*. The National Academies.

Phillips, J. L. (n.d.). Information liability: The possible chilling effect of tort claims against producers of geographic information systems data. *Florida State University Law Review*, *26*, 743.

Purdy, R. (2010). Using earth observation technologies for better regulatory compliance and enforcement of environmental laws. *Journal of Environmental Law*, 22(1). 43 U.S.C. 2801–2811.

Routledge Handbook of Commercial Space Law (ed. Smith, L.J., Baumann, Ingo and Wintermuth, S-G) (2023).

United Nations Global Geospatial Information Management (UNGGIM). (n.d.). *Compendium on the licensing of geospatial information*.

Index

For Product Safety Concerns and Information please contact our EU
representative GPSR@taylorandfrancis.com
Taylor & Francis Verlag GmbH, Kaufingerstraße 24, 80331 München, Germany

www.ingramcontent.com/pod-product-compliance
Ingram Content Group UK Ltd.
Pitfield, Milton Keynes, MK11 3LW, UK
UKHW020001200926
475702UK00015B/2414
9781032360287